ACTION GUIDE

THINK
AND
GROW
RICH!

ACTION GUIDE

An Official Publication of the
NAPOLEON HILL FOUNDATION

Sound Wisdom

P.O. Box 310

Shippensburg, PA 17257-0310

For more information on foreign distributors, call 717-532-2122.

Or reach us on the Internet: www.soundwisdom.com.

While efforts have been made to verify information contained in this publication, neither the author nor the publisher assumes any responsibility for errors, inaccuracies, or omissions.

While this publication is chock-full of useful, practical information; it is not intended to be legal or accounting advice. All readers are advised to seek competent lawyers and accountants to follow laws and regulations that may apply to specific situations.

The reader of this publication assumes responsibility for the use of the information. The author and publisher assume no responsibility or liability whatsoever on the behalf of the reader of this publication.

Cover Design by Eileen Rockwell

Interior Design by Terry Clifton

ISBN 13 TP: 978-1-937879-90-7

For Worldwide Distribution, Printed in the U.S.A.

4 5 6 / 21

CONTENTS

Introduction

THOUGHTS ARE THINGS

"There was never anything that did not proceed from a thought."
—RALPH WALDO EMERSON

THIS WORKBOOK IS DESIGNED to stimulate your mind and your dreams and your desire to achieve, to go beyond where you are now in financial resources, meaningful relationships, and career aspirations. Based on thirteen proven and practical principles, or steps, you will have the tools and encouragement to advance in life—the sky is the limit. And it all begins with how you think.

Truly, "Thoughts are things," and powerful things at that, when they are mixed with definiteness of purpose, persistence, and a *burning desire* for their translation into riches, or other material objects.

There is a true story about Edwin C. Barnes that is worth introducing to you straight away. He is an excellent example of how he allowed his thoughts to motivate him toward pursuing his goal and then enjoyed the abundant financial and personal rewards of his efforts.

Edwin C. Barnes discovered the truth that people really can think and grow rich. He didn't discover this overnight. It came little by little, beginning with a burning desire of his to work with the great inventor, Thomas Edison. It was a definite desire. Barnes wanted to work *with* Edison, not *for* him.

He presented himself at Mr. Edison's laboratory and announced that he had come to go into business with the inventor. It could not have been the young man's appearance that got him his start in the Edison office, for that was definitely against him. It was what he *thought* that counted.

Months went by, and apparently nothing substantial was happening toward achieving his goal. But something important *was* happening in Barnes' mind. He was constantly intensifying his desire to become the business associate of Edison. Psychologists have correctly said that when you are truly ready for something, it puts in an appearance. Barnes was ready for a business association with Edison; moreover, *he was determined to remain ready until he got what he wanted.*

Eventually that business alliance became a reality and it was in operation for more than thirty years. Out of it, Barnes made himself rich in money, but he did something infinitely greater, he proved that people really can *Think and Grow Rich.*

How much actual cash that original *desire* of Barnes' was worth to him, there is no way of knowing. Perhaps it brought him $2 or $3 million; but the amount, whatever it was, is insignificant compared with the greater asset he acquired in the form of definite knowledge that an intangible impulse of thought can be transmuted into its physical counterpart by the application of known principles.

One sound idea is all that you need to achieve success. The principles described in this book contain the best and most practical of all that is known concerning ways and means of creating useful ideas.

Before we go any further in our approach to the description of these principles, you are entitled to receive this important suggestion: *When riches begin to come, they come so quickly, in such great abundance, that you may wonder where they had been hiding during all those lean years.* This is an astounding statement, and all the more so when we take into consideration the popular belief that riches come only to those who work hard and long.

Riches begin with a state of mind.

When you begin to *think and grow rich,* you will observe that riches begin with a state of mind and definiteness of purpose. You ought to be interested in knowing how to acquire the state of mind that will attract riches. I spent twenty-five years in research, analyzing more than 25,000 people, because I, too, wanted to know how wealthy people become that way.

Observe very closely that as soon as you master the principles of this philosophy and begin to follow the instructions for applying those principles, your financial status will begin to improve, and everything you touch will begin to transmute itself into an asset for your benefit. Impossible? Not at all!

One of the main weaknesses of humankind is the average person's familiarity with the word "impossible." We know all the rules that will *not* work. We know all the things that *cannot* be done. This book was written for those who seek the rules that have made others successful, and are willing to stake everything on those rules.

Success comes to those who become *success conscious.* Failure comes to those who indifferently allow themselves to become *failure conscious.* The object of this book is to help all who seek it, to learn the art of changing their minds from *failure consciousness* to *success consciousness.*

Success comes to those who become *success conscious.*

Another weakness found in altogether too many people, is the habit of measuring everything and everyone by their own impressions and beliefs. Some who will read this will believe that no one can *think and grow rich*. They cannot think in terms of riches, because their thought habits have been steeped in poverty, want, misery, failure, and defeat.

When William Ernest Henley wrote the prophetic lines, "I am the master of my fate, I am the captain of my soul," he informed us all that we are the masters of our fate and the captains of our souls—*because we have the power to control our thoughts.*

In the ether in which this little earth floats, in which we move and have our being, is a form of energy moving at an inconceivably high rate of vibration, and that ether is filled with a form of universal power that *adapts* itself to the nature of the thoughts we hold in our minds; and *influences* us, in natural ways, to transmute our thoughts into their physical equivalent. This power makes no attempt to discriminate between destructive thoughts and constructive thoughts, and it will urge us to translate into physical reality thoughts of poverty, just as quickly as thoughts of riches.

Our brains become magnetized with the dominating thoughts that we hold in our minds; and, by means with which no one is familiar, these "magnets" attract to us the forces, the people, and the circumstances of life that harmonize with the nature of our dominating thoughts.

Before we can accumulate riches in great abundance, we must magnetize our minds with intense *desire* for riches, and we must become "money conscious" until the *desire* for money drives us to create definite plans for acquiring it.

When Edwin C. Barnes climbed down from the freight train in Orange, New Jersey, he may have resembled a tramp, but his thoughts were those of a king! As he made his way from the railroad tracks to Thomas A. Edison's office, his mind was at work. He saw himself standing in Edison's presence. He heard himself asking Mr. Edison for an opportunity to carry out the one consuming obsession of his life, a burning desire to become the business associate of the great inventor.

With definite desire, your dominating dream in life will become a reality.

Barnes' desire was not a hope! It was not a wish! It was a keen, pulsating *desire*, which transcended everything else. It was *definite*.

The desire was not new when he approached Edison. It had been Barnes' dominating desire for a long time. In the beginning, when the desire first appeared in his mind, it may have been, probably was, only a wish, but it was no mere wish when he appeared before Edison with it.

A few years later, Edwin C. Barnes again stood before Edison, in the same office where he first met the inventor. This time his *desire* had been translated into reality. He was in business with Edison. *The dominating dream of his life had become a reality.* People who knew Barnes envied him, because of the "break" life yielded him. They saw him in the days of his triumph, without taking the trouble to investigate the cause of his success.

Barnes succeeded because he chose a definite goal, placed all his energy, all his will-power, all his effort, everything into that goal. He did not become the partner of Edison the day he arrived. He was content to start in the most menial work, as long as it provided an opportunity to take even one step toward his cherished goal.

It is a remarkable illustration of the power of a *definite desire*. Barnes achieved his goal because he wanted to be a business associate of Mr. Edison more than he wanted anything else. He created a plan to attain that purpose. He burned all bridges behind him. He stood by his *desire* until it became the dominating obsession of his life—and—finally, a fact.

IMPORTANT SUMMARY POINTS

- All things begin with a thought—positive and negative.

- Riches begin with a state of mind and a definite purpose.

- Learning how to control your thoughts is even more valuable than the money it will bring you.

- Destructive thoughts will translate into reality just as surely as positive thoughts. It is important to choose your thoughts carefully.

TAKE ACTION

1. Do you allow any and all thoughts to occupy your mind? What steps can you take to control the thoughts that flow into and out of your mind?

_____

_____

_____

_____

_____

_____

_____

_____

_____

_____

2. How passionate is your desire to "think and grow rich"? How can you generate more desire for the things you want?

_____

_____
_____
_____
_____
_____
_____
_____
_____
_____
_____

3. Have you a burning desire that you never voiced aloud? Is there a desire that is so big you are afraid to even consider it seriously? Write that desire down on paper and then say it out loud. What is the first step you will take to make that desire a reality?

_____
_____
_____
_____
_____
_____
_____
_____
_____

Chapter 1

DESIRE:
THE STARTING POINT OF ALL ACHIEVEMENT

"A creative man is motivated by the desire to achieve, not by the desire to beat others."
—AYN RAND

First Step toward Riches

A long while ago, a great warrior faced a situation that made it necessary for him to make a decision which ensured his success on the battlefield. He was about to send his armies against a powerful foe, whose men outnumbered his own. He loaded his soldiers into boats, sailed to the enemy's country, unloaded soldiers and equipment, then gave the order to burn the ships that had carried them.

Addressing his men before the first battle, he said, "You see the boats going up in smoke. That means we cannot leave these shores alive unless we win! We now have no choice—we win—or we perish!" They won.

Every person who wins in any undertaking must be willing to burn their ships and cut all sources of retreat. Only by so doing can we be sure of maintaining the state of mind known as a *burning desire to win,* essential to success.

Wishing will not bring riches.

Every human being who reaches the age of understanding of the purpose of money, wishes for it. Wishing will not bring riches. But desiring riches with a state of mind that becomes an obsession, then planning definite ways and means to acquire riches, and backing those plans with persistence which does not recognize failure, will bring riches.

Those who become "money conscious" accumulate great riches. "Money consciousness" means that the mind has become so thoroughly saturated with the *desire* for money, that the person can see him or herself already in possession of it.

The steps call for no "hard labor." They call for little to no sacrifice. They do not require you to become ridiculous or credulous. To apply them calls for no great amount of education. But the successful application of these six steps does call for sufficient imagination to enable you to see and to understand that accumulation of money cannot be left to chance, good fortune, and luck. You must realize that all who have accumulated great fortunes, first did a certain amount of *dreaming, hoping, wishing, desiring, and planning* before they acquired money.

If you do not see great riches in your imagination, you will never see them in your bank balance.

Tolerance and an open mind are practical necessities of the dreamer of today. Those who are afraid of new ideas are doomed before they start. Never has there been a time more favorable to pioneers than the present. True, there is no wild and woolly West to be conquered; but there are vast business, financial, industrial, and cyberspace worlds to be explored, remolded, and redirected along new and better lines.

Awake, arise, and assert yourself, you world dreamer. Your star is now ascending. The world's economic crises brought the opportunity you have been waiting for. It taught people humility, tolerance, and open-mindedness.

The world is filled with an abundance of opportunity that the dreamers of the past never knew.

We who are in this race for riches, should be encouraged to know that this changed world in which we live is demanding new ideas, new ways of doing things, new leaders, new inventions, new methods of teaching, new methods of marketing, new books, new literature, new features for the radio, new ideas for moving pictures. Back of all this demand for new and better things, there are three qualities you must possess to win: 1) definiteness of purpose, 2) knowledge of what you want, and 3) a burning *desire* to possess it.

The recession marked the death of one age, and the birth of another. This changed world requires practical dreamers who can and will put their dreams into action. The practical dreamers have always been, and always will be the pattern makers of civilization.

A *burning desire to be and to do* is the starting point from which the dreamer must take off. Dreams are not born of indifference, laziness, or lack of ambition.

How can you harness and use the power of desire? This question has been answered through this and the subsequent chapters of this book. This message is going out to the world during tumultuous times worldwide. It is reasonable to presume that the message may come to the attention of many who have been wounded by the economic chaos, those who have lost their fortunes, others who have lost their positions, and great numbers who must reorganize their plans and stage a comeback. To all these I wish to convey the thought that all achievement, no matter what may be its nature, or its purpose, must begin with an intense burning desire for something definite.

All achievement begins with an intense burning desire for something definite.

Through some strange and powerful principle of "mental chemistry" never divulged, Nature wraps up in the impulse of strong desire "that certain something" that recognizes no such word as "impossible," and accepts no such reality as failure.

There is a difference between *wishing* for a thing and being *ready* to receive it. No one is ready for a thing, until he believes he can acquire it. The state of mind must be *belief*, not mere hope or wish. Open-mindedness is essential for belief. Closed minds do not inspire faith, courage, and belief.

Remember, no more effort is required to aim high in life, to demand abundance and prosperity, than is required to accept misery and poverty.

IMPORTANT SUMMARY POINTS

- Success begins with setting a definite goal.

- Write a clear, concise statement of your definite major purpose, be specific. (If it's monetary, write the exact amount you wish to acquire and set an exact date for when you want to acquire it.)

- Read your statement aloud twice per day.

- If you do not see great riches in your imagination, you will never see them in your bank balance.

- Never in the history of the United States has there been so great an opportunity for practical dreamers as now exists.

- The world we live in is demanding new ideas, new inventions, and new ways of doing things. This means opportunity. To capitalize on these ever-emerging opportunities, you must possess a definiteness of purpose, the knowledge of what you want, and a burning desire to possess it.

- A burning desire to be and to do is the starting point from which you the dreamer must take off.

TAKE ACTION

The method by which *desire* for riches can be transmuted into its financial equivalent, consists of six definite, practical steps:

1. Fix in your mind the exact amount of money you desire. It is not sufficient merely to say "I want plenty of money." Be definite as to the amount. (There is a psychological reason for definiteness that is described in a subsequent chapter.)

2. Determine exactly what you intend to give in return for the money you desire. (There is no such reality as something for nothing.)

3. Establish a definite date when you intend to possess the money you desire.

4.   Create a definite plan for carrying out your desire, and begin at once, whether you are ready or not, to put this plan into action.

5.   Write out a clear, concise statement of the amount of money you intend to acquire, name the time limit for its acquisition, state what you intend to give in return for the money, and describe clearly the plan through which you intend to accumulate it.

6.   Read your written statement aloud, twice daily, once just before retiring at night, and once after waking up in the morning. *As you read, see and feel and believe yourself already in possession of the money.*

It is important that you follow the instructions described in these six steps. It is especially important that you observe and follow the instructions in the sixth paragraph. You may complain that is impossible for you to "see yourself in possession of money" before you actually have it, but here is where a *burning desire* will come to your aid. If you truly *desire* money so keenly that your desire is an obsession, you will have no difficulty in convincing yourself that you will acquire it. The object is to want money, and to become so determined to have it that you *convince* yourself you will have it.

Chapter 2

FAITH:
SECOND STEP TOWARD RICHES

*"Take the first step in faith. You don't have to see
the whole staircase, just take the first step."*
—MARTIN LUTHER KING JR.

Faith: Visualization of and Belief in Attainment of Desire

Faith is a state of mind which may be induced, or created, by affirmation or repeated instructions to the subconscious mind through the principle of auto-suggestion.

As an illustration, consider the purpose for which you are, presumably, reading this book. The object is, naturally, to acquire the ability to transmute the intangible thought impulse of desire into its physical counterpart, money. By following the instructions laid down in the chapters on auto-suggestion and the subconscious mind, summarized in the chapter on auto-suggestion, you may *convince* the subconscious mind that you believe you will receive what you ask, and it will act upon that belief, which your subconscious mind passes back to you in the form of "faith," followed by definite plans for procuring what you desire.

The method by which you develop *faith*, where it does not already exist, is extremely difficult to describe, almost as difficult, in fact, as it would be to describe the color red to a blind man who has never seen color and has nothing to compare with what you describe to him. Faith is a state of mind you may develop after you have mastered the thirteen principles, or steps, discussed throughout this book. Faith is a state of mind that develops voluntarily through application and use of these principles.

Repetition of affirmation of orders to your subconscious mind is the only known method of voluntary development of the emotion of faith.

The meaning of faith may be made clearer through the following explanation of the way people sometimes become criminals. Stated in the words of a famous criminologist, "When men first come into contact with crime, they abhor it. If they remain in contact with crime for a time, they become accustomed to it, and endure it. If they remain in contact with it long enough, they finally embrace it, and become influenced by it."

This is the equivalent of saying that any impulse of thought that is repeatedly passed on to the subconscious mind is, finally, accepted and acted upon by the subconscious mind, which proceeds to translate that impulse into its physical equivalent, by the most practical procedure available.

In connection with this, consider the statement: *All thoughts that have been emotionalized, (given feeling) and mixed with faith, begin immediately to translate themselves into their physical equivalent or counterpart.*

The emotions, or the "feeling" portion of thoughts, are the factors that give thoughts vitality, life, and action. The emotions of faith, love, and sex, when mixed with any thought impulse, give it greater action than any of these emotions can do singly.

Emotionalized thoughts mixed with faith immediately translate physically.

Not only thought impulses that have been mixed with faith, but those mixed with any positive or negative emotions may reach and influence the subconscious mind.

From this statement, you will understand that the subconscious mind will translate into its physical equivalent, a thought impulse of a negative or destructive nature, just as readily as it will act upon thought impulses of a positive or constructive nature. This accounts for the strange phenomenon so many millions of people experience, referred to as "misfortune" or "bad luck."

There are millions of people who *believe* themselves "doomed" to poverty and failure, because of some strange force over which they *believe* they have no control. They are the creators of their own "misfortunes" because of this negative *belief*, which is picked up by the subconscious mind and translated into its physical equivalent.

All through the ages, the religionists have admonished struggling humanity to "Have faith" in this, that, and the other dogma or creed, but they have failed to tell people *how* to have faith. They have not stated that "Faith is a state of mind, and that it may be induced by self-suggestion."

Faith is a state of mind induced by self-suggestion.

Always remember to have faith in yourself; faith in the Infinite. And:

- Faith is the "eternal elixir" that gives life, power, and action to the impulse of thought!

- The previous bullet point sentence is worth reading a second time, and a third, and a fourth. It is worth reading aloud!

- Faith is the starting point of all accumulation of riches!

- Faith is the basis of all "miracles" and all mysteries that cannot be analyzed by the rules of science!

- Faith is the only known antidote for failure!

- Faith is the element, the "chemical" that, when mixed with prayer, gives you direct communication with Infinite Intelligence.

- Faith is the element that transforms the ordinary vibration of thought, created by the finite mind of humans, into the spiritual equivalent.

- Faith is the only agency through which the cosmic force of Infinite Intelligence can be harnessed and used by you.

IMPORTANT SUMMARY POINTS

- Faith is a state of mind that may be induced, or created, by affirmation or repeated instructions to the subconscious mind.

- All thoughts emotionalized and mixed with faith immediately begin to translate into a physical equivalent or counterpart.

- Your belief, or faith, is the element that determines the action of your subconscious mind.

- There are millions of people who *believe* themselves "doomed" to poverty and failure, because of some strange force over which they *believe* they have no control. They are the creators of their own misfortune.

- Faith is the starting point of all accumulation of riches.

- Faith gives life, power, and action to the impulse of thought.

- The subconscious mind translates into reality a thought driven by fear—just as readily as it will translate into reality a thought driven by faith.

TAKE ACTION

The following is a Self-Confidence Formula. There are five affirmations that are important to absorb into your mindset and then apply to your everyday life. Find a quiet, private place and write each component of the formula; then speak each one aloud—confidently.

1. I know that I have the ability to achieve the object of my Definite Purpose in life, therefore, I *demand* of myself persistent, continuous action toward its attainment, and I here and now promise to render such action.

_____

_____

_____

_____

_____

_____

_____

_____

_____

_____

_____

2. I realize the dominating thoughts of my mind will eventually reproduce them-
    selves in outward, physical action, and gradually transform themselves into
    physical reality; therefore, I will concentrate my thoughts for thirty minutes daily,
    upon the task of thinking of the person I intend to become, thereby creating in
    my mind a clear mental picture of that person.

_____

_____

_____

_____

_____

_____

_____

_____

_____

_____

3. I know through the principle of auto-suggestion, any desire that I persistently hold in my mind will eventually seek expression through some practical means of attaining the object back of it; therefore, I will devote ten minutes daily to demanding of myself the development of self-confidence.

_____

_____

_____

_____

_____

_____

_____

_____

_____

4. I have clearly written down a description of my definite chief aim in life, and I will never stop trying, until I have developed sufficient self-confidence for its attainment.

_____

_____

_____

_____

_____

_____

_____

_____

_____

5. I fully realize that no wealth or position can long endure unless built upon truth and justice; therefore, I will engage in no transaction that does not benefit all whom it affects. I will succeed by attracting to myself the forces I wish to use and the cooperation of other people. I will induce others to serve me, because of my willingness to serve others. I will eliminate hatred, envy, jealousy, selfishness, and cynicism, by developing love for all humanity, because I know that a negative attitude toward others can never bring me success. I will cause others to believe in me, because I will believe in them, and in myself.

_____

_____

_____

_____

_____

_____

_____

_____

I will sign my name to this formula, commit it to memory, and repeat it aloud once a day, with full _faith_ that it will gradually influence my _thoughts and actions_ so that I will become a self-reliant and successful person.

Sign Here: _____

The basis of this formula is a law of nature that no one has yet been able to explain. It has baffled scientists of all ages. The psychologists have named this law "auto-suggestion," and let it go at that.

Chapter 3

AUTO-SUGGESTION:
THIRD STEP TOWARD RICHES

Auto-Suggestion: The Medium for Influencing the Subconscious Mind

Auto-suggestion is a term that applies to all suggestions and all self-administered stimuli that reach a person's mind through the five senses. Stated another way, auto-suggestion is self-suggestion. It is the agency of communication between that part of the mind where conscious thought takes place, and that which serves as the seat of action for the subconscious mind.

Through the dominating thoughts we permit to remain in our conscious mind (whether these thoughts are negative or positive is immaterial), the principle of auto-suggestion voluntarily reaches the subconscious mind and influences it with these thoughts.

No thought, whether negative or positive, *can enter the subconscious mind without the aid of the principle of auto-suggestion,* with the exception of thoughts picked up from the ether. Stated differently, all sense impressions perceived through the five senses are stopped by the *conscious* thinking mind, and may be either passed on to the subconscious mind or rejected. The conscious faculty serves as an outer guard to the approach of the subconscious.

Nature has built us so that we have *absolute control* over the material that reaches our subconscious minds, through our five senses, although this is not meant to be constructed

27

as a statement that we always *exercise* this control. In the great majority of instances, we do *not* exercise it, which explains why so many people go through life in poverty.

The subconscious mind resembles a fertile garden spot in which weeds will grow in abundance, if the seeds of more desirable crops are not sown. Auto-suggestion is the agency of control through which an individual may voluntarily feed his or her subconscious mind on thoughts of a creative nature, or, by neglect, permit thoughts of a destructive nature to find their way into this rich garden of the mind.

You were instructed, in the steps described in Chapter 1 on Desire, to read *aloud* twice daily the *written* statement of your *desire for money*, and to *see and feel* yourself *already in possession* of the money! By following these instructions, you communicate the object of your *desire* directly to your *subconscious* mind in a spirit of absolute *faith*. Through repetition of this procedure, you voluntarily create thought habits that are favorable to your efforts to transmute desire into its monetary equivalent.

Go back to the steps described in the Take Action section in Chapter 1, and read them again, very carefully, before you proceed further. Then when you come to Chapter 6, Organized Planning, read very carefully the four instructions for the organization of your Master Mind group. By comparing these two sets of instructions with what has been stated about auto-suggestion, you, of course, will see that the instructions involve the application of the principle of auto-suggestion.

Remember, therefore, when reading aloud the statement of your desire (through which you are endeavoring to develop a "money consciousness"), that the *mere reading of the words is of no consequence unless you mix emotion or feeling with your words*. If you repeat a million times the famous Emil Coué formula, "Day by day, in every way, I am getting better and better," without mixing emotion and faith with your words, you will experience no desirable results. Your subconscious mind recognizes and acts upon *only* thoughts that have been well mixed with emotion or feeling.

Your subconscious mind recognizes and acts upon only the thoughts that have been well-mixed with emotion or feeling.

This is a fact of such importance it is repeated in practically every chapter. The main reason the majority of people who try to apply the principle of auto-suggestion get no desirable results is because they don't understand that their subconscious minds recognize and act upon *only* thoughts that have been well mixed with emotion or feeling.

Plain, unemotional words do not influence the subconscious mind. You will get no appreciable results until you learn to reach your subconscious mind with thoughts or spoken words that have been well emotionalized with belief.

Do not become discouraged if you cannot control and direct your emotions the first time you try. Remember, there is no such possibility as something for nothing. The ability to reach and influence your subconscious mind has its price, and you must pay that price.

You cannot cheat, even if you desire to do so. The price of ability to influence your subconscious mind is everlasting *persistence* in applying the principles described in Chapters 1 through 13. You cannot develop the desired ability for a lower price. *You alone* must decide whether or not the reward you are striving for (the "money conscious"), is worth the price you must pay for it in effort.

Wisdom and "cleverness" alone will not attract and retain money, except in a few very rare instances where the law of averages favors the attraction of money through these sources. The method of attracting money described in this workbook, does not depend upon the law of averages.

Your ability to use the principle of auto-suggestion will depend, very largely, upon your capacity to *concentrate* on a given *desire* until that desire becomes a burning obsession. When you begin to carry out the Take Action instructions described in Chapter 1, you need to tap into the power of *concentration*.

Your subconscious mind takes in and acts on all repeated orders given in a spirit of absolute *faith*.

For example, when you "fix in your own mind the *exact* amount of money you desire," hold your thoughts on that amount of money by concentrating, or fixating your attention, with your eyes closed, until you can *actually see* the physical appearance of the money. Do this at least once each day. As you go through these exercises, *see yourself actually in possession* of the money!

Here is a most significant fact—the subconscious mind takes any orders given it in a spirit of absolute *faith*, and acts upon those orders, although the orders often have to be presented over and over again, through repetition, before they are interpreted by the subconscious mind.

IMPORTANT SUMMARY POINTS

- No thought, whether negative or positive, can enter the subconscious mind without the aid of auto-suggestion.

- The ability to reach and influence your subconscious mind has a price you must pay. The price is everlasting persistence in applying the thirteen steps.

- The subconscious mind takes any orders given it in a spirit of absolute faith and acts on those orders.

- Imagine yourself already in possession of your definite desire.

- Place your written statement where you can see it night and morning. Read it just before going to bed and again upon awaking, until you have it memorized.

- You can become the master of yourself and your environment because you have the power to influence your subconscious mind.

TAKE ACTION

The instructions given in Chapter 1 are summarized and blended with the principles covered in this chapter. Take these suggestions seriously and implement as quickly as possible:

1. Go to some quiet spot (preferably in bed at night) where you will not be disturbed or interrupted, close your eyes, and repeat aloud (so you can hear your own words) the written statement of the amount of money you intend to accumulate, the time limit for its accumulation, and a description of the service or merchandise you intend to give in return for the money. As you carry out these instructions, see yourself already in possession of the money.

   For example, suppose you intend to accumulate $50,000 by the first of January, five years from now, by giving personal services as a salesperson in return for the money. Your written statement of your purpose should be similar to the following:

   "By January 1, 20__, I will have in my possession $50,000 that will come to me in various amounts from time to time during the interim. In return for this money, I will give the most efficient service possible, rendering the fullest possible quantity and the best possible quality of service as a salesperson of (describe the service or merchandise you intend to sell).

"I believe that I will have this money in my possession. My faith is so strong that I can now see this money before my eyes. I can touch it with my hands. It is now awaiting transfer to me at the time and in the proportion that I deliver the service I intend to render in return for it. I am awaiting a plan by which to accumulate this money, and I will follow that plan when it is received."

2.   Repeat this program night and morning until you can see (in your imagination) the money you intend to accumulate.

3.   Place a written copy of your statement where you can see it at night and in the morning. Read it just before retiring and upon arising until you have it memorized.

Remember, as you carry out these instructions, you are applying the principle of auto-suggestion for the purpose of giving orders to your subconscious mind. Remember, also, that your subconscious mind will act *only* upon instructions that are emotionalized and handed over to it with "feeling."

Faith is the strongest, and most productive of the emotions. Follow the instructions given in Chapter 2 on *Faith*. These instructions may at first seem abstract. Do not let this disturb you. Follow the instructions, no matter how abstract or impractical they may, at first, appear to be. The time will soon come, if you do as you have been instructed in spirit as well as in act, when a whole new universe of power will unfold to you.

Skepticism, in connection with *all* new ideas, is characteristic of all human beings. But if you follow the instructions outlined, your skepticism will soon be replaced by belief, and this, in turn, will soon become crystallized into *absolute faith*. Then you will have arrived at the point where you may truly say, "I am the master of my fate, I am the captain of my soul!"

Chapter 4

SPECIALIZED KNOWLEDGE:
FOURTH STEP TOWARD RICHES

Specialized Knowledge: Personal Experiences or Observations

There are two kinds of knowledge: general and specialized. General knowledge, no matter how great in quantity or variety it may be, is of little use in the accumulation of money. The faculties of the great universities possess, in the aggregate, practically every form of general knowledge known to civilization. Most of the professors have little or no money. They specialize in teaching knowledge, but they do not specialize in the organization or the use of knowledge.

Knowledge will not attract money unless it is organized and intelligently directed through *practical plans of action to the definite end* of the accumulation of money. Lack of understanding this fact has been the source of confusion to millions of people who falsely believe that "Knowledge is power." It is nothing of the sort! Knowledge is only potential power. It becomes power only when, and if, it is organized into definite plans of action and directed to a definite end.

This "missing link" in all systems of education known to civilization today, may be found in the failure of educational institutions to teach their students *how to organize and use knowledge after they acquire it.*

Before you can be sure of your ability to transmute *desire* into its monetary equivalent, you will require specialized knowledge of the service, merchandise, or profession you intend to offer in return for fortune. Perhaps you may need much more specialized knowledge than you have the ability or the inclination to acquire; if true, you can bridge your weakness through your Master Mind group.

Andrew Carnegie stated that he, personally, knew nothing about the technical end of the steel business; moreover, he did not particularly care to know anything about it. The specialized knowledge he required for the manufacture and marketing of steel, he found available through the individual units of his Master Mind group.

The accumulation of great fortunes calls for *power* that is acquired through highly organized and intelligently directed specialized knowledge; but that knowledge does not, necessarily, have to be in the possession of the person who accumulates the fortune.

The preceding paragraph should give hope and encouragement to everyone with ambition to accumulate a fortune, who has not possessed the necessary "education" to supply such specialized knowledge as required. Many people go through life suffering from "inferiority complexes," because they are not "educated." The person who can organize and direct a Master Mind group who possesses knowledge useful in the accumulation of money, is just as much a person of education as anyone in the group.

Remember this—if you suffer from a feeling of inferiority because your schooling has been limited, Thomas A. Edison had only three months of "schooling" during his entire life. He did not lack education, neither did he die poor. And Henry Ford, founder of Ford Motor Company, had less than a sixth grade "schooling" but he managed to become enormously influential in the industrial world, introducing revolutionary new mass-production methods and the first moving assembly line for cars, which greatly benefited him financially.

As knowledge is acquired, it must be organized and put into use, for a definite purpose, through practical plans.

Specialized knowledge is among the most plentiful and cheapest forms of service. First of all, decide the sort of specialized knowledge you require, and the purpose for which it is needed. To a large extent, your major purpose in life, the goal toward which you are working, will help determine what knowledge you need. With this question settled, your next move is to acquire accurate information concerning dependable sources of knowledge. The more important of these are:

- Your own experience and education

- Experience and education available through cooperation of others (Master Mind Alliance)

- Colleges and universities

- Public libraries (books and periodicals in which may be found all the knowledge organized by civilization)

- Special training courses (night schools and home study schools in particular)

- Internet resources

As knowledge is acquired, it must be organized and put into use, for a definite purpose, through practical plans. Knowledge has no value except what can be gained from its application toward some worthy end. This is one reason why college degrees are not valued more highly. They represent nothing but miscellaneous knowledge.

If you contemplate additional schooling, first determine the purpose for which you want the knowledge you are seeking, then learn where this particular sort of knowledge can be obtained, from reliable sources.

Successful people, in all callings, never stop acquiring specialized knowledge related to their major purpose, business, or profession. Those who are not successful usually make the mistake of believing that the knowledge-acquiring period ends when they finish school. The truth is that schooling does little more than to put a person in the way of learning how to acquire practical knowledge.

The *basis of all ideas* is specialized knowledge. Unfortunately, for those who do not find riches in abundance, specialized knowledge is more abundant and more easily acquired than *ideas*. Because of this very truth, there is a universal demand and an ever-increasing opportunity for the person capable of helping men and women sell their personal services advantageously.

Capability means *imagination*, the one quality needed to combine specialized knowledge with *ideas*, in the form of *organized plans* designed to yield riches.

If you have a keen imagination, the next chapter may present you with an idea sufficient to serve as the beginning of the riches you desire. Remember, the *idea*, the thought, is the main thing. Specialized knowledge may be found just around the corner—any corner!

IMPORTANT SUMMARY POINTS

- There are two kinds of knowledge: general and specialized.

- General knowledge is of little use in the accumulation of money.

- Knowledge will not attract money unless it is organized and intelligently directed through practical plans of action to the definite end of accumulation of money.

- The missing link in all systems of education known to civilization today is how to organize and use knowledge after it is acquired.

- Decide what sort of specialized knowledge you require and the purpose for which it is needed. Then acquire it.

- Knowledge has no value except what can be gained from its application toward some worthy end.

- Successful people, in all callings, never stop acquiring specialized knowledge related to their major purpose, business, or profession.

TAKE ACTION

1. Have you determined the *purpose* and *need* for gaining specific knowledge?

_____

_____

2. What kind of specialized knowledge do you need to realize your goal(s)? List your ideas for potential sources of specialized knowledge below:

_____

_____

_____

_____

_____

_____
_____
_____
_____
_____

3. Have you researched and found a reliable, credible source for gaining that particular sort of knowledge?

_____
_____
_____
_____
_____
_____
_____
_____

4. What specific steps are you going to take to begin acquiring the specific knowledge you need to succeed? Write down the steps; write down the timeline; then take action.

_____
_____
_____

Chapter 5

IMAGINATION:
FIFTH STEP TOWARD RICHES

Imagination: The Workshop of the Mind

The imagination is literally the workshop where all plans are fashioned. The impulse, the *desire*, is given shape, form, and *action* through the aid of the imaginative faculty of the mind.

It has been said that people can create anything they can imagine. Of all the ages of civilization, this is the most favorable for the development of the imagination, because it is an age of rapid change. On every hand we can contact stimuli that develops the imagination.

Through the aid of our imaginative faculty, we have discovered and harnessed more of Nature's forces during the past fifty years than during the entire history of the human race. We have conquered the air so completely that the birds are a poor match for flying. We have harnessed the ether and made it serve as a means of instantaneous communication with any part of the world.

We have analyzed and weighed the sun at a distance of millions of miles and determined, through the aid of *imagination*, the elements of which it consists. We have discovered that our brains are broadcasting and receiving stations for the vibration of thought. And we are beginning now to learn how to make practical use of this discovery.

Two Forms of Imagination

The imaginative faculty functions in two forms: "synthetic imagination" and "creative imagination."

Synthetic imagination: Through synthetic imagination, we can arrange old concepts, ideas, or plans into new combinations. This faculty creates nothing. It merely works with the material of experience, education, and observation with which it is fed. It is the faculty used most by the inventor, with the exception of the "genius" who draws upon the creative imagination, when he or she cannot solve a problem through synthetic imagination.

Creative imagination: Through the faculty of creative imagination, the finite mind of humans has direct communication with Infinite Intelligence. It is the faculty through which "hunches" and "inspirations" are received. It is by this faculty that all basic or new ideas are handed over to people.

It is through this faculty that thought vibrations from the minds of others are received. It is through this faculty that one individual may "tune in" or communicate with the sub-conscious minds of other people.

The creative imagination works automatically in the manner described in subsequent pages. This faculty functions *only* when the conscious mind is vibrating at an exceedingly rapid rate; as for example, when the conscious mind is stimulated through the emotion of a strong desire. The creative faculty becomes more alert, more receptive to vibrations from the sources mentioned, in proportion to its development through *use*. This statement is significant! Ponder over it before reading on.

Keep in mind as you follow these thirteen steps, or principles, that the entire story will be complete only when you have *mastered, assimilated, and begun to make use* of them all.

The great leaders of business, industry, finance, and the great artists, musicians, poets, and writers became great because they developed the faculty of creative imagination. Both the synthetic and creative faculties of imagination become more alert with use, just as any muscle or organ of the body develops through use.

Desire is only a thought, an impulse. It is nebulous and ephemeral. It is abstract and of no value until it has been transformed into its physical counterpart. The synthetic imagination is the one used most frequently in the process of transforming the impulse of *desire* into money. But keep in mind that you may face circumstances and situations that demand use of the creative imagination as well.

Transforming the intangible desire into the tangible reality of money requires a plan.

Your imaginative faculty may have become weak through inaction. It can be revived and made alert through *use*. This faculty does not die, though it may become quiescent through lack of use.

Transformation of the *intangible impulse of desire into the tangible reality of money* calls for the use of a plan, or plans. These plans must be formed with the aid of the imagination, and mainly, with the synthetic imagination faculty.

Begin at once to put your imagination to work on the building of a plan, or plans, for the transformation of your desire into money. Detailed instructions for the building of plans have been given in almost every chapter of the *Think and Grow Rich* book. Carry out the instructions best suited to your needs, and reduce your plan to writing, if you have not already done so.

IMPORTANT SUMMARY POINTS

- The impulse, the desire, is given shape, form, and action through the aid of the imaginative faculty of the mind.

- It has been said that people can create anything they can imagine.

- Of all the ages of civilization, this is the most favorable for the development of the imagination, because it is an age of rapid change.

- Your only limitation, within reason, lies in your development and use of your imagination.

- Synthetic imagination is rearranging old ideas, concepts, and plans into new combinations.

- Creative imagination is the inspiration of new ideas.

- The story of practically every great fortune starts with the day when a creator of ideas and a seller of ideas got together and worked in harmony.

TAKE ACTION

1. Are you in the process of transforming the impulse of desire into money? Write your step-by-step process and its progress.

_____

_____

_____

_____

_____

_____

_____

_____

2. Has your imaginative faculty become weak through inaction? Do you need to revive it by using it? What action will you take to revive it?

3. Are you developing your synthetic imagination? It is most often used in the process of converting desire into money.

_____

_____

_____

4. Transforming the intangible impulse of desire into the tangible reality of money requires a plan, or plans. Have you a plan for this transformation? Write a cogent, practical plan and then act on it.

_____

_____

_____

_____

_____

_____

_____

_____

_____

Chapter 6

ORGANIZED PLANNING:
SIXTH STEP TOWARD RICHES

The Crystallization of Desire into Action

You have learned that everything humankind creates or acquires begins in the form of *desire*, that desire is taken on the first lap of its journey, from the abstract to the concrete, into the workshop of the *imagination*, where *plans* for its transition are created and organized.

In Chapter 1, you were instructed to take six definite, practical steps as your first move in translating the desire for money into its monetary equivalent. One of these steps is the formation of a *definite*, practical plan, or plans, through which this transformation may be made—including forming a Master Mind group.

The following are four steps to build practical plans:

1. Ally yourself with a group of as many people as you may need for the creation and carrying out of your plan, or plans, for the accumulation of money—making use of the Master Mind principle described in a later chapter. (Compliance with this instruction is absolutely essential. Do not neglect it.)

2. Before forming your Master Mind alliance, decide what advantages and benefits you may offer the individual members of your group in return for their cooperation. No one will work indefinitely without some form of compensation. No intelligent person will either request or expect another to work without adequate compensation, although this may not always be in the form of money.

3. Arrange to meet with the members of your Master Mind group at least twice a week, more often if possible, until you have jointly perfected the necessary plan, or plans, for the accumulation of money.

4. Maintain *perfect harmony* between yourself and every member of your Master Mind group. If you fail to carry out this instruction to the letter, you may meet with failure. The Master Mind principle cannot obtain where perfect harmony does not prevail.

Keep in mind these facts:

First. You are engaged in an undertaking of major importance to you. To be sure of success, you must have faultless plans.

Second. You must have the advantage of the experience, education, native ability, and imagination of other minds. This is in harmony with the methods followed by every person who has accumulated a great fortune.

No individual has sufficient experience, education, native ability, and knowledge to ensure the accumulation of a great fortune without the cooperation of other people. Every plan you adopt, in your endeavor to accumulate wealth, should be the joint creation of yourself and every other member of your Master Mind group. You may originate your own plans, either in whole or in part, but *ensure that your plans are reviewed and approved by the member of your Master Mind alliance.*

If the first plan you adopt does not work successfully, replace it with a new plan; if this new plan fails to work, replace it in turn with still another, and so on, *until you find a plan that does work.* Right here is the point where the majority of people meet with failure—their lack of *persistence* to create new plans to take the place of those that fail.

No one can accumulate money without practical and workable plans.

The most intelligent person living cannot succeed in accumulating money—nor in any other undertaking—without practical and workable plans. Keep this fact in mind: when your plans fail, that temporary defeat is not permanent failure. It may only mean that your plans have not been sound. Build other plans. Start all over again.

Thomas A. Edison "failed" ten thousand times before he perfected the incandescent electric light bulb. That is—he met with temporary defeat ten thousand times before his efforts were crowned with success.

Temporary defeat should mean only one thing, the certain knowledge that there is something wrong with your plan. Millions of people go through life in misery and poverty because they lack a sound plan through which to accumulate happiness and a fortune.

Your achievements can be no greater than your plans are sound.

Henry Ford accumulated a fortune not because of his superior mind, but because he adopted and followed a *sound plan*. A thousand people could be pointed out as having a better education than Ford's, yet those thousand live in poverty because they do not possess the right plan for the accumulation of money.

IMPORTANT SUMMARY POINTS

- If the first plan you adopt does not work successfully, replace it with a new plan; keep trying and replacing until it works.

- The most intelligent person living cannot succeed in accumulating money—nor in any other undertaking—without practical and workable plans.

- Millions of people go through life in misery and poverty, because they lack a sound plan through which to accumulate a fortune.

- Your achievements can be no greater than your plans are sound.

TAKE ACTION

There are ten major causes of failure in leadership. Carefully read the following and then write about experiences of each that have caused you trouble in the past and what you will do to prevent them from being problems in the future:

1. *Inability to organize details.* Efficient leadership calls for ability to organize and master details. No genuine leader is ever "too busy" to do anything required in his or her capacity as the leader. Whether a leader or follower, when you admit you are "too busy" to change a plan or give attention to an emergency, you admit inefficiency. The successful leader must be the master of all details connected with the position. That means, of course, acquiring the habit of relegating details to capable colleagues.

_____
_____
_____
_____

2. *Unwillingness to render humble service.* Truly great leaders are willing, when occasion demands, to perform any sort of labor they would ask someone else to perform.

_____
_____
_____
_____
_____
_____
_____
_____
_____
_____

3. *Expectation of pay for what they "know" instead of what they "do" with what they know.* The world does not pay people for what they "know." It pays them for what they *do,* or induce others to do.

_____
_____
_____
_____

---

4. *Fear of competition from followers.* The leader who fears that one of the followers wants his or her position is practically sure to realize that fear sooner or later. On the other hand, the able leader trains understudies so to delegate tasks. Only in this way may a leader multiply and prepare to be at many places, giving attention to many things at one time. It is an eternal truth that people receive more pay for their *ability to get others to perform,* than they could possibly earn by their own efforts. An efficient leader may, through knowledge of the job and the magnetism of personality, greatly increase the efficiency of others, and induce them to render more service and better service than they could render without his or her aid.

---

5. *Lack of imagination.* Without imagination, the leader is incapable of meeting emergencies and creating plans to guide the followers efficiently.

6. *Selfishness.* The leader who claims all the honor for the work of the followers is sure to be met with resentment. The really great leader claims none of the honors. He or she is content to see the honors, when there are any, go to the followers, knowing that most people work harder for commendation and recognition than they will for money alone.

_____
_____
_____
_____

7. *Intemperance.* Followers do not respect an intemperate leader. Moreover, intemperance in any of its various forms, destroys the endurance and the vitality of all who indulge in it.

_____
_____
_____
_____
_____
_____
_____
_____
_____

8. *Disloyalty.* Perhaps disloyalty should have been placed at the head of the list. The leader who is not loyal or trustworthy to associates, those above and those below, cannot long maintain leadership. Disloyalty marks a person as contemptable. Lack of loyalty is one of the major causes of failure in every walk of life.

_____
_____
_____
_____

---

9. *Emphasis of the "authority" of leadership.* The efficient leader leads by encouraging, not by trying to instill fear in the hearts of the followers. The leader who tries to impress followers with "authority" is placed within the category of "leadership through force." If a leader is a real leader, he will have no need to advertise that fact except by good conduct—sympathy, understanding, fairness, and a demonstration that he or she knows the job.

10. *Emphasis of title.* The competent leader requires no "title" to gain the respect of followers. The leader who makes too much over a title generally has little else to emphasize. The doors to the office of the real leader are open to all who wish to enter, and his or her working quarters are free from formality or ostentation.

Chapter 7

DECISION:
SEVENTH STEP TOWARD RICHES

Accurate analysis of more than 25,000 men and women who had experienced failure, disclosed the fact that *lack of decision* was near the top of the list of the thirty major causes of *failure*. This is no mere statement of a theory—it is a fact.

Procrastination, the opposite of *decision,* is a common enemy that almost every man and woman must conquer.

You will have an opportunity to test your capacity to reach quick and definite *decisions* when you finish reading this book and are ready to put into *action* the principles you learned.

Analysis of several hundred people who had *accumulated fortunes* well beyond the million-dollar mark disclosed the fact that every one of them had the habit of *reaching decisions promptly,* and of changing those decisions *slowly,* if and when they needed to be changed.

People who *fail* to accumulate money, without exception, have the habit of reaching decisions, *if at all,* very slowly, and of changing those decisions quickly and often.

One of Henry Ford's most outstanding qualities was his habit of reaching decisions quickly and definitely, and changing them slowly. This quality is so pronounced in Mr.

Ford, that it gave him the reputation of being obstinate. This quality prompted Mr. Ford to continue to manufacture his famous Model "T" (the world's ugliest car), when all of his advisors, and many of the purchasers of the car, were urging him to change it.

Make a habit of reaching decisions quickly and definitely, and changing them slowly.

Perhaps, Mr. Ford delayed too long in making the change, but the other side of the story is that Mr. Ford's firmness of decision yielded a huge fortune, before the change in model became necessary. There is little doubt that Mr. Ford's habit of definiteness of decision assumes the proportion of obstinacy, but this quality is preferable to slowness in reaching decisions and quickness in changing them.

The majority of people who fail to accumulate money sufficient for their needs are generally easily influenced by the "opinions" of others. They permit newspapers and "gossiping" neighbors to do their "thinking" for them. Opinions are the cheapest commodities on earth. Everyone has a flock of opinions ready to be wished upon anyone who will accept them. If you are influenced by opinions when you reach decisions, you will not succeed in any undertaking, much less in that of transmuting your own desire into money.

If you are influenced by the opinions of others, you will have no desire of your own.

When you begin to put into practice the principles described here, reach your own decisions and follow them. Take no one into your confidence, except the members of your Master Mind group; and be very sure in your selection of this group that you choose only those who will be in complete agreement and harmony with your purpose.

Close friends and relatives, while not meaning to do so, often handicap someone with unsolicited opinions and sometimes ridicule, which is meant to be humorous. Thousands of men and women carry inferiority complexes with them all through life because some well-meaning, but ignorant person destroyed their confidence through opinions or ridicule.

You have a brain and mind of your own. *Use it* to reach your own decisions. If you need facts or information from other people to enable you to reach decisions, as you probably will in many instances, acquire these facts or secure the information you need quietly, without disclosing your purpose.

It is characteristic of people who have only a smattering or a veneer of knowledge to try to give the impression that they have much knowledge. Such people generally do *too much talking and too little listening*. Keep your eyes and ears wide open—and your mouth closed if you wish to acquire the habit of prompt decision making. Those who talk too much do little else. If you talk more than you listen, you not only deprive yourself of many opportunities to accumulate useful knowledge, but you also disclose your *plans and purposes* to people who will take great delight in defeating you, because they envy you.

The value of decisions depends upon the courage required to render them.

The value of decisions depends upon the courage required to render them. The great decisions, which served as the foundation of civilization, were reached by assuming great risks, which often meant the possibility of death.

Abraham Lincoln's decision to issue his famous Proclamation of Emancipation, freeing the slaves, was rendered with full understanding that his act would turn thousands of friends and political supporters against him. He knew, too, that the carrying out of that proclamation would mean death to thousands of men on the battlefield. In the end, it cost Lincoln his life. That required courage.

Socrates' decision to drink the cup of poison, rather than compromise in his personal belief was a decision of courage. It turned time ahead a thousand years, and gave to people then unborn, the right to freedom of thought and of speech.

But the greatest decision of all time, as far as any American citizen is concerned, was reached in Philadelphia, July 4, 1776, when fifty-six men signed their names to a document that they well knew would bring freedom to all Americans, or leave every one of the fifty-six hanging from the gallows!

Analyze the events that led to the Declaration of Independence and you will be convinced that this nation, which now holds a position of commanding respect and power among all nations of the world, was born of a *decision* created by a Master Mind group, consisting of fifty-six men.

Note the fact that it was their *decision* that ensured the success of George Washington's armies, because the spirit of that decision was in the heart of every soldier who fought with him, and served as a spiritual power that recognizes no such thing as failure.

Note also (with great personal benefit), that the power that gave this nation its freedom is the selfsame power that must be used by every individual who becomes self-determining. This power is made up of the principles described in this workbook. It is not difficult to detect, in the story of the Declaration of Independence, at least six of these principles: *desire, decision, faith, persistence, the Master Mind, and organized planning.*

Throughout this philosophy is found the suggestion that *thought*, backed by strong *desire*, has a tendency to transmute itself into its physical equivalent. Before going further, I wish to leave with you the suggestion that you may find in this story, and in the story of the organization of the United States Steel Corporation, a perfect description of the method by which thought makes this astounding transformation.

In your search for the secret of the method, do not look for a miracle, because you will not find it. You will find only the eternal laws of Nature. These laws are available to every person who has the *faith* and *courage* to use them. They may be used to bring freedom to a nation, or to accumulate riches. There is no charge except the time necessary to understand and appropriate them.

Those who reach decisions promptly and definitely know what they want and generally get it. Leaders in every walk of life decide quickly and firmly. That is the major reason why they are leaders. The world has the habit of making room for those whose words and actions show they know where they are going.

Those who reach decisions promptly and definitely generally get what they want.

Indecision is a habit that usually begins when a person is young. The habit takes on permanency as the youth goes through grade school, high school, and even through college, without definiteness of purpose. The major weakness of all educational systems is that they neither teach nor encourage the habit of definite decision.

It would be beneficial if no college would permit the enrollment of any student, unless and until the student declared his or her major purpose in matriculating. It would be of still greater benefit if every student who enters school were compelled to accept training in the habit of decision making and forced to pass a satisfactory examination on this subject before being permitted to advance.

The habit of indecision acquired because of the deficiencies in our school systems goes with the student into the occupation chosen—if in fact an occupation is chosen. Generally, the youth just out of school seeks any job, taking the first one found. I venture to say that ninety-eight out of every hundred people working for wages today, are in the positions they hold because they lacked the definiteness of decision to plan a definite position and the knowledge of how to choose an employer.

Definiteness of decision always requires courage, sometimes very great courage. The fifty-six men who signed the Declaration of Independence staked their lives on the decision to affix their signatures to that document. The person who reaches a definite decision to procure a particular job and make life pay the price asked does not stake his or her life on that decision; the decision is staked on *economic freedom*.

Financial independence, riches, desirable business and professional positions are not within reach of the person who neglects or refuses to *expect, plan, and demand* these things. The person who desires riches in the same spirit that Samuel Adams desired freedom for the Colonies is sure to accumulate wealth.

In the chapter on Organized Planning in *Think and Grow Rich*, you will find complete instructions for marketing every type of personal services. You will find also detailed information on how to choose the employer you prefer, and the particular job you desire. These instructions will be of no value to you unless you definitely decide to organize them into a plan of action.

IMPORTANT SUMMARY POINTS

- Procrastination, the opposite of decision, is a common enemy that everyone must conquer.

- Analysis of several hundred millionaires showed that every one of them had the habit of making decisions promptly and changing them slowly, if at all.

- The majority of people who fail to accumulate money sufficient for their needs are generally easily influenced by the opinions of others.

- If you are influenced by the opinion of others, you will have no desire of your own.

- You have a brain and mind of your own—use it to reach your own decisions.

- Keep your eyes and ears open and your mouth closed if you want to acquire the habit of reaching prompt decisions.

- The value of decisions often depends on the courage required to make them. The great decisions that serve as the foundation of civilization were reached by assuming great risks, which often meant the possibility of death.

- Financial independence, riches, desirable business, and professional positions are not within reach of the person who neglects or refuses to expect, plan, and demand these things.

TAKE ACTION

The major causes of failure are listed here. Evaluate each described failure and write down your reaction to each. How many of these are holding *you* back?

1. *Unfavorable heredity background.* There is little, if anything, that can be done for people who are born with a deficiency in brain power. This philosophy offers one method of bridging this weakness—through the aid of the Master Mind. Observe with profit, however, that this is the *only* one of the thirty causes of failure that may not be easily corrected by any individual.

_____

_____

2. *Lack of a well-defined purpose in life.* There is no hope of success for the person who does not have a central purpose or definite goal at which to aim. Ninety-eight out of every hundred analyzed had no such aim. Perhaps this was the major cause of their failure.

_____

_____

_____

_____

_____

_____

_____

3. *Insufficient education.* This handicap may be overcome with comparative ease. Experience has proven that the best-educated people are often those who are known as "self-made" or self educated. It takes more than a college degree to make an educated person. Anyone who is educated has learned to get whatever he or she wants in life without violating the rights of others. Education consists, not so much of knowledge, but of knowledge effectively and persistently applied. People are paid not merely for what they know, but more particularly for what they do with what they know.

_____

_____

_____

_____

4.   *Lack of self-discipline.* Discipline comes through self-control. This means that you must control all negative qualities. Before you can control conditions, you must first control yourself. Self-mastery is the hardest job you will ever tackle. If you do not conquer self, you will be conquered by self. You may see at one and the same time both your best friend and your greatest enemy, by stepping in front of a mirror.

----

5.   *Ill health.* No person may enjoy outstanding success without good health. Many of the causes of ill health are subject to mastery and control.

----

6. *Procrastination.* Procrastination is one of the most common causes of failure. "Old Man Procrastination" stands within the shadow of every human being, waiting his opportunity to spoil your chances of success. Most of us go through life as failures because we are waiting for the "time to be right" to start doing something worthwhile. Do not wait. The time will never be "just right." Start where you stand and work with whatever tools you may have at your command; better tools will be found as you go along.

    _____

    _____

    _____

    _____

7. *Lack of persistence.* Most of us are good "starters" but poor "finishers" of everything we begin. Moreover, people are prone to give up at the first signs of defeat. There is no substitute for persistence. The person who makes persistence the watch-word discovers that "Old Man Failure" finally becomes tired and departs. Failure cannot cope with persistence.

    _____

    _____

    _____

    _____

8. *Negative personality.* There is no hope of success for the person who repels people with a negative personality. Success comes through the application of power, and power is attained through the cooperative efforts of other people. A negative personality will not induce cooperation.

    _____

    _____

    _____

    _____

---

9. *Uncontrolled desire for "something for nothing."* The gambling instinct drives millions of people to failure. Evidence of this may be found in a variety of current events as well as a study of the Wall Street crash of 1929, during which millions of people tried to make money by gambling on stock margins.

---

10. *Lack of a well-defined power of decision.* People who succeed reach decisions promptly and change them, if at all, very slowly. People who fail reach decisions, if at all, very slowly and change them frequently and quickly. Indecision and procrastination are twins. Where one is found, the other may usually be found also. Kill off this pair before they completely hog-tie you to the treadmill of failure.

---

11. *One or more of the six basic fears.* These fears have been analyzed for you in Chapter 14. They must be mastered before you can market your services effectively.

----

12. *Overcaution.* The person who takes no chances generally has to take whatever is left when others are through choosing. Overcaution is as bad as under-caution. Both are extremes to be guarded against. Life itself is filled with the element of chance.

----

13. *Wrong selection of business associates.* This is one of the most common causes of failure in business. In marketing personal services, you should use great care to select an employer who will be an inspiration and who is intelligent and successful. We emulate those with whom we associate most closely. Pick an employer worth emulating.

----

14. *Superstition and prejudice.* Superstition is a form of fear. It is also a sign of ignorance. People who succeed keep open minds and are afraid of nothing.

----

15. *Wrong selection of vocation.* No one can succeed in a line of endeavor that you dislike. The most essential step in the marketing of personal services is that of selecting an occupation into which you can throw yourself wholeheartedly.

16. *Lack of concentration of effort.* The "jack-of-all-trades" seldom is good at any. Concentrate all of your efforts on *one definite chief aim.*

17. *The habit of indiscriminate spending.* The spend-thrift cannot succeed, mainly because he or she stands eternally in fear of poverty. Form the habit of systematic saving by putting aside a definite percentage of your income. Money in the bank gives you a very safe foundation of courage when bargaining for the sale of personal services. Without money, you must take what one is offered, and be glad to get it.

18. *Lack of enthusiasm.* Without enthusiasm, you cannot be convincing. Moreover, enthusiasm is contagious; and the person who has it, under control, is generally welcome in any group of people.

19. *Intolerance.* The person with a "closed" mind on any subject seldom gets ahead. Intolerance means that the person has stopped acquiring knowledge. The most damaging forms of intolerance are those connected with religious, racial, and political differences of opinion.

20. *Intemperance.* The most damaging forms of intemperance are connected with eating, strong drink, and sexual activities. Overindulgence in any of these is fatal to success.

---

21. *Inability to cooperate with others.* More people lose their positions and their big opportunities in life because of the inability to cooperate than for all other reasons combined. It is a fault that no well-informed business person or leader will tolerate.

---

22. *Possession of power that was not acquired through self-effort* (sons and daughters of wealthy parents and others who inherit money that they did not earn). Power in the hands of someone who did not acquire it gradually is often fatal to success. Quick riches are more dangerous than poverty.

_____

_____

_____

_____

_____

_____

23. *Intentional dishonesty.* There is no substitute for honesty. Someone may be temporarily dishonest by force of circumstances, over which he or she has no control, without permanent damage. But there is no hope for the person who is dishonest by choice. Sooner or later, the deeds will catch up and the person will pay by loss of reputation, and perhaps even loss of liberty.

_____

_____

_____

_____

_____

24. *Egotism and vanity.* These two qualities serve as red lights that warn others to keep away. They are fatal to success.

_____

_____

_____

_____

_____

25. *Guessing instead of thinking.* Most people are too indifferent or lazy to acquire facts with which to think accurately. They prefer to act on opinions created by guesswork or snap judgments.

_____

_____

_____

_____

_____

_____

_____

26. *Lack of capital.* This is a common cause of failure among those who start out in business for the first time, without sufficient reserve of capital to absorb the shock of their mistakes, and to carry them over until they have established a reputation.

_____

_____

_____

_____

_____

_____

Chapter 8

PERSISTENCE:
EIGHTH STEP TOWARD RICHES

Persistence: The Sustained Effort Necessary to Induce Faith

Persistence is an essential factor in the procedure of transmuting *desire* into its monetary equivalent. The basis of persistence is the *power of will*.

Willpower and desire, when properly combined, makes an irresistible pair. People who accumulate great fortunes are generally known as cold-blooded sometimes ruthless. Often they are misunderstood. What they have is willpower, which they mix with persistence, and place back of their desires to ensure the attainment of their objectives.

Henry Ford has been generally misunderstood to be ruthless and cold-blooded. This misconception grew out of Ford's habit of following through in all of his plans with persistence. The majority of people are ready to throw their aims and purposes overboard and give up at the first sign of opposition or misfortune. A few carry on despite all opposition until they attain their goal. These few are the Fords, Carnegies, Rockefellers, and Edisons, and many modern-day successful men and women.

There may be no heroic connotation to the word "persistence," but the quality is to the character of humans what carbon is to steel. The building of a fortune, generally, involves the application of the entire thirteen factors of this philosophy. These principles, or steps, must be understood; they must be applied with persistence by all who wish to accumulate money.

If you are following this workbook with the intention of applying the knowledge it conveys, your first test of your persistence will come when you begin to take action with the six steps described in the first chapter. Unless you are one of the two out of every hundred who already have a *definite goal* at which you are aiming, and a *definite plan* for its attainment, you may read the instructions and then go about your daily routine—never complying with the instructions.

Lack of persistence can be conquered; it depends entirely on your intensity of desire.

The author is checking you up at this point, because lack of persistence is one of the major causes of failure. Moreover, experience with thousands of people has proved that lack of persistence is a weakness common to the majority of people. It is a weakness, though, that can be overcome by effort. The ease with which lack of persistence may be conquered depends entirely on your intensity of desire.

The starting point of all achievement is desire. Keep this constantly in mind. Weak desires bring weak results, just as a small amount of fire makes a small amount of heat. If you find yourself lacking in persistence, this weakness may be remedied by building a stronger fire under your desires.

Continue to read through to the end of the workbook, then go back to Chapter 1 and start immediately to carry out the instructions given in connection with the six steps in the Take Action section. The eagerness with which you follow these instructions will indicate clearly how much, or how little, you really desire to accumulate money. If you find that you are indifferent, you may be sure that you have not yet acquired the "money consciousness" you must possess before you can be sure of accumulating a fortune.

Fortunes gravitate to people whose minds have been prepared to "attract" them, just as surely as water gravitates toward the ocean. In the *Think and Grow Rich* book and this workbook may be found all the stimuli necessary to attune any normal mind to the vibrations that will attract the object of your desires.

If you find you are weak in persistence, center your attention on the instructions contained in the next chapter that focuses on the power of the Master Mind. Surround yourself with a Master Mind group; and through the cooperative efforts of the members of that group, you can develop persistence. You will find additional instructions for the development of persistence in the chapters on auto-suggestion (Chapter 3) and the subconscious mind (Chapter 11). Follow the instructions outlined in these chapters until your habit nature hands over to your subconscious mind, a clear picture of the object of your desire. From that point on, you will not be handicapped by lack of persistence.

Your subconscious mind works continuously—while you are awake and while you are asleep.

Spasmodic, or occasional effort to apply the rules will be of no value to you. To get results, you must apply all of the rules until their application becomes a fixed habit with you. In no other way can you develop the necessary money consciousness.

Without persistence, you will be defeated, even before you start. With persistence, you will win.

Poverty is attracted to anyone whose mind is favorable to it, as money is attracted to anyone whose mind has been deliberately prepared to attract it, and through the same laws. Poverty consciousness will voluntarily seize the mind that is not occupied with the money consciousness. A poverty consciousness develops without conscious application of habits favorable to it. The money consciousness must be created to order, unless born with such a consciousness.

Catch the full significance of the statements in the preceding paragraph, and you will understand the importance of persistence in the accumulation of a fortune. Without persistence, you will be defeated, even before you start. With persistence, you will win.

If you have ever experienced a nightmare, you will realize the value of persistence. You are lying in bed, half awake, with a feeling that you are about to smother. You are unable to turn over, or to move a muscle. You realize that you *must begin to regain control* over your muscles. Through persistent effort of willpower, you finally manage to move the fingers of one hand. By continuing to move your fingers, you extend your control to the muscles of one arm, until you can lift it. Then you gain control of the other arm in the same manner. You finally gain control over the muscles of one leg, and then extend it to the other leg. Then, with one supreme effort of will, you regain complete control over your muscular system, and *snap* out of your nightmare. The trick has been turned step by step.

You may find it necessary to *snap* out of your mental inertia through a similar procedure—moving slowly at first, then increasing your speed until you gain complete control over your will. Be persistent no matter how slowly you may, at first, have to move. With persistence comes success.

With persistence comes success.

If you select your Master Mind group with care, you will have in it at least one person who will aid you in the development of persistence. Some who have accumulated great fortunes, did so because of necessity. They developed the habit of persistence because they were so closely driven by circumstances that they had to become persistent.

There is no substitute for persistence! It cannot be supplanted by any other quality! Remember this, and it will hearten you, in the beginning, when the going may seem difficult and slow.

Those who have cultivated the habit of persistence enjoy insurance against failure. No matter how many times they are defeated, they finally arrive toward the top of the ladder. Sometimes it appears that there is a hidden Guide whose duty is to test people through all sorts of discouraging experiences. Those who pick themselves up after defeat and keep trying, arrive; and the world cries, "Bravo! I knew you could do it!" The hidden Guide lets no one enjoy great achievement without passing the persistence test. Those who can't take it, simply do not make the grade.

Those who can "take it" are bountifully rewarded for their persistence. They receive, as their compensation, whatever goal they are pursuing. That is not all! They receive something infinitely more important than material compensation—the knowledge that "Every failure brings with it the seed of an equivalent advantage."

IMPORTANT SUMMARY POINTS

- The basis of persistence is the power of will.

- The majority of people are ready to throw their aims and purposes overboard and give up at the first sign of opposition or misfortune.

- There may be no heroic connotation to the word "persistence," but the quality is to the character of humans what carbon is to steel.

- The lack of persistence is one of the major causes of failure.

- If you find yourself lacking in persistence, this weakness may be remedied by building a stronger fire under your desires.

- Without persistence, you will be defeated before you begin. With persistence, you will win.

- There is no substitute for persistence.

- Those who cultivate the habit of persistence enjoy insurance against failure.

TAKE ACTION

Take action to develop a habit of persistence by studying and following these four simple steps. They call for no great amount of intelligence and no particular amount of education—only time and effort:

1. A definite purpose backed with a burning desire for its fulfillment.

2. A definite plan expressed with continuous action.

3. A mind closed tightly against all negative and discouraging influences, including negative suggestions of family, friends, and acquaintances.

4. A friendly alliance with one or more people who will encourage you to follow through with both your plan and purpose.

Chapter 9

POWER OF THE MASTER MIND:
NINTH STEP TOWARD RICHES

The Driving Force

The Master Mind may be defined as: "Coordination of knowledge and effort, in a spirit of harmony between two or more people, for the attainment of a definite purpose."

To have great power, you must avail yourself to the Master Mind principle. In a preceding chapter, instructions were given for the creation of *plans* for the purpose of translating *desire* into its monetary equivalent. If you carry out these instructions with *persistence* and intelligence, and use discrimination in the selection of your Master Mind group, your objective will have been halfway reached, even before you begin to recognize it.

So you may better understand the "intangible" potentialities of power available to you, through a properly chosen Master Mind group, we will here explain the two characteristics of the Master Mind principle, one of which is *economic* in nature, and the other *psychic*. The economic feature is obvious. Economic advantages may be created by people who surround themselves with the advice, counsel, and personal cooperation of a group willing to lend you wholehearted aid, in a spirit of *perfect harmony*. This form of cooperative alliance has been the basis of nearly every great fortune. Your understanding of this great truth may definitely determine your financial status.

Two characteristics of the Master Mind principle: *economic* and *psychic.*

The psychic phase of the Master Mind principle is much more abstract, much more difficult to comprehend, because it references spiritual forces with which the human race, as a whole, is not well acquainted. You may catch a significant suggestion from this statement: "No two minds ever come together without, thereby, creating a third, invisible, intangible force which may be likened to a third mind."

Keep in mind the fact that there are only two known elements in the whole universe—energy and matter. It is a well-known fact that matter may be broken down into units of molecules, atoms, and electrons. There are units of matter that may be isolated, separated, and analyzed.

Likewise, there are units of energy.

The human mind is a form of energy, a part of it being spiritual in nature. When the minds of two people are coordinated in a *spirit of harmony*, the spiritual units of energy of each mind form an affinity, which constitutes the psychic phase of the Master Mind.

The Master Mind principle, or rather the economic feature of it, was first called to my attention by Andrew Carnegie. Discovery of this principle was responsible for the choice of my life's work.

Mr. Carnegie's Master Mind group consisted of approximately fifty men with whom he surrounded himself for the *definite purpose* of manufacturing and marketing steel. He attributed his entire fortune to the *power* he accumulated through this Master Mind.

Analyze the record of anyone who has accumulated a great fortune, and many of those who have accumulated modest fortunes, and you will find that they have either consciously or unconsciously employed the Master Mind principle.

Great power and success can be accumulated with the Master Mind principle.

Energy is Nature's universal set of building blocks, out of which is constructed every material thing in the universe, including humankind, and every form of animal and vegetable life. Through a process that only Nature completely understands, energy is translated into matter.

Nature's building blocks are available to humankind in the energy involved in *thinking!* Your brain can be compared to an electric battery. It absorbs energy from the ether, which permeates every atom of matter and fills the entire universe.

It is a well-known fact that a group of electric batteries will provide more energy than a single battery. It is also a well-known fact that an individual battery will provide energy in proportion to the number and capacity of the cells it contains.

The brain functions in a similar fashion. This accounts for the fact that some brains are more efficient than others, and leads to this significant statement—a group of brains coordinated (or connected) in a spirit of harmony, will provide more thought-energy than a single brain, just as a group of electric batteries will provide more energy than a single battery.

Through this metaphor it becomes immediately obvious that the Master Mind principle holds the secret of the *power* wielded by people who surround themselves with other people of brains.

There follows, now, another statement that will lead still nearer to an understanding of the psychic phase of the Master Mind principle: When a group of individual brains are coordinated and function in harmony, the increased energy created through that alliance becomes available to every individual brain in the group.

People take on the nature and the habits and the power of thought of those with whom they associate in a spirit of sympathy and harmony.

Henry Ford whipped poverty, illiteracy, and ignorance by allying himself with great minds, whose vibrations of thought he absorbed into his own mind. Through his association with Edison, Burbank, Burroughs, and Firestone, Mr. Ford added to his own brain power the sum and substance of the intelligence, experience, knowledge, and spiritual forces of these four men. Moreover, he appropriated and made use of the Master Mind principle through the methods of procedure described in this workbook. *This principle is available to you!*

IMPORTANT SUMMARY POINTS

- No two minds ever come together without creating a third invisible, intangible force, likened to a third mind.

- When the minds of two people are coordinated in a spirit of harmony, the spiritual energy of each mind forms an affinity, which constitutes the psychic phase of the Master Mind.

- Analyze the record of anyone who has accumulated a great fortune, and you will find that they have either consciously or unconsciously employed the Master Mind principle.

- A group of brains coordinated in a spirit of harmony will provide more thought-energy than a single brain.

- The Master Mind principle holds the secret of the power wielded by people who surround themselves with other people of brains.

- People take on the nature and the habits and the power of thought of those with whom they associate in a spirit of sympathy and harmony.

TAKE ACTION

Because *power* is essential for success in the accumulation of money, *plans* are inert and useless without sufficient *power* to translate them into *action*. And because *power* is defined as "organized and intelligently directed knowledge," it is important to examine the sources of knowledge—then put that *knowledge into action:*

- *Infinite intelligence.* This source of knowledge is absorbed through the procedure described in Chapter 11, with the aid of Creative Imagination.

- *Accumulated experience.* The accumulated experience of a person (or that portion of it which has been organized and recorded), may be found in any well-equipped public library and from credible sources on the Internet. An important part of this accumulated experience is taught in public schools and colleges, where it has been classified and organized.

- *Experiment and research.* In the field of science, and in practically every other walk of life, people are gathering, classifying, and organizing new facts daily.

This is the source to turn to when knowledge is not available through "accumulated experience." Here, too, the Creative Imagination must often be used.

Knowledge may be acquired from any of these three sources and converted into *power* by organizing it into definite *plans* and by expressing those plans in terms of *action*.

Examination of these three major sources of knowledge will readily disclose the difficulty you may have if dependent on your efforts alone in assembling knowledge and expressing it through definite plans in terms of action. If your plans are comprehensive, and if they contemplate large proportions, you must induce others to cooperate before you can inject into them the necessary element of power. Describe below your ideal mastermind group and why you chose each member.

_____

_____

_____

_____

_____

_____

_____

_____

_____

_____

_____

_____

_____

Chapter 10

THE MYSTERY OF SEX:
TENTH STEP TOWARD RICHES

The Mystery of Sex Transmutation

The meaning of the word "transmute" is, in simple language, "the changing, or transferring of one element, or form of energy, into another."

The emotion of sex brings into being a state of mind. Because of ignorance, this state of mind is generally associated with the physical, and because of improper influences to which most people have been subjected in acquiring knowledge of sex, things essentially physical have highly biased the mind. This chapter focuses on men, but women can glean much knowledge and insight from it as well.

Behind the emotion of sex is the possibility of three constructive potentialities:

1. The perpetuation of humankind.

2. The maintenance of health—as a therapeutic agency, it has no equal.

3   The transformation of mediocrity into genius through transmutation.

Sex transmutation is simple and easily explained. It means the switching of the mind from thoughts of physical expression, to thoughts of some other nature.

Sex desire is the most powerful of human desires. When driven by this desire, men, particularly, develop keenness of imagination, courage, willpower, persistence, and creative ability unknown to them at other times. So strong and impelling is the desire for sexual contact that men freely run the risk of life and reputation to indulge it. When harnessed and redirected along other lines, this motivating force maintains all of its attributes of keenness of imagination, courage, etc., which may be used as powerful creative forces in literature, art, or in any other profession or calling, including, of course, the accumulation of riches.

The transmutation of sex energy calls for the exercise of willpower, to be sure, but the reward is worth the effort. The desire for sexual expression is inborn and natural. The desire cannot and should not be submerged or eliminated. But it should be given an outlet through forms of expression that enrich the body, mind, and spirit. If not given this form of outlet, through transmutation, it will seek outlets through purely physical channels.

Give sex energy an outlet through expressions that enrich the body, mind, and spirit.

A river may be dammed and its water controlled for a time, but eventually it will force an outlet. The same is true of the emotion of sex. It may be submerged and controlled for a time, but its very nature causes it to be ever seeking means of expression. If it is not transmuted into some creative effort, it will find a less worthy outlet.

Fortunate, indeed, is the person who has discovered how to give sex emotion an outlet through some form of creative effort, for by that discovery the person has been lifted to the status of a genius.

Scientific research has disclosed these significant facts:

1. The men of greatest achievement are men with highly developed sex natures; men who have learned the art of sex transmutation.

2. The men who have accumulated great fortunes and achieved outstanding recognition in literature, art, industry, architecture, and the professions, were motivated by the influence of a woman.

The research from which these astounding discoveries were made went back through the pages of biography and history for more than two thousand years. Wherever there was evidence available in connection with the lives of men and women of great achievement, it indicated most convincingly that they possessed highly developed sex natures.

The emotion of sex is an "irresistible force" against which there can be no such opposition as an "immovable body." When driven by this emotion, men become gifted with a super power for action. Understand this truth, and you will catch the significance of the statement that sex transmutation will lift you to the status of a genius.

The emotion of sex contains the secret of creative ability.

Destroy the sex glands, whether in man or beast, and you have removed the major source of action. For proof of this, observe what happens to any animal after it has been castrated. A bull becomes as docile as a cow after it has been altered sexually. Sex alteration takes out of the male, whether man or beast, all the fight that was in him. Sex alteration of the female has the same effect.

The Ten Mind Stimuli

The human mind responds to stimuli, through which it may be "keyed up" to high rates of vibration, known as enthusiasm, creative imagination, intense desire, etc. The stimuli to which the mind responds most freely are:

1. The desire for sex expression

2. Love

3. A burning desire for fame, power, or financial gain, money

4. Music

5. Friendship

6. A Master Alliance based on the harmony of two or more people who ally themselves for spiritual or temporal advancement

7. Mutual suffering, such as that experienced by people who are persecuted

8. Auto-suggestion

9. Fear

10. Narcotics and alcohol

The desire for sex expression comes at the head of the list of stimuli, which most effectively "step-up" the vibrations of the mind and start the "wheels" of physical action. Eight of these stimuli are natural and constructive. Two are destructive.

The list is presented for the purpose of enabling you to make a comparative study of the major sources of mind stimulation. It is readily seen that the emotion of sex is, by great odds, the most intense and powerful of all mind stimuli.

IMPORTANT SUMMARY POINTS

- Sex transmutation means switching the mind from thoughts of physical expression to thoughts of some other nature.

- Sex desire is the most powerful human desire.

- When driven by sex desire, people develop keenness of imagination, courage, willpower, persistence, and creative ability unknown to them at other times.

- The transmutation of sex energy calls for the exercise of willpower, but the reward is worth the effort.

- The world is ruled by human emotions.

- Intemperance in sex habits is just as detrimental as intemperance in habits of drinking alcohol and eating.

TAKE ACTION

Are you taking advantage of the power of sex energy by transmuting it in constructive ways? This power can be communicated to others through:

1. *A handshake.* The touch of the hand indicates, instantly, the presence of magnetism, or the lack of it.

2. *Your tone of voice.* Magnetism, or sex energy, is the factor with which the voice may be colored, or made musical and charming.

3. *Your posture and the way you carry yourself.* Highly sexed people move briskly, and with grace and ease.

4. *Vibrations of thought.* Highly sexed people mix the emotion of sex with their thoughts and influence those around them.

5. *Body adornment.* People who are highly sexed are usually very careful about their personal appearance. They usually select a clothing style becoming to their personality, physique, complexion, etc.

6. *When employing sales associates, capable sales managers look for the quality of personal magnetism as the first requirement.* People who lack sex energy will never become enthusiastic nor inspire others with enthusiasm—and *enthusiasm is one of the most important requisites in salesmanship, no matter what you are selling.* Highly successful sales people attain the status of "master" because they either consciously or unconsciously transmute the energy of sex into sales enthusiasm!

Have you acquired this trait? Write down some ideas about what sex transmutation means to you and how you can apply it in your life.

Chapter 11

THE SUBCONSCIOUS MIND:
ELEVENTH STEP TOWARD RICHES

The Connecting Link

The subconscious mind consists of a field of consciousness in which every impulse of thought that reaches the objective mind, through any of the five senses, is classified and recorded, and from which thoughts may be recalled or withdrawn, as letters may be taken from a filing cabinet.

The subconscious mind receives and files sense impressions or thoughts, regardless of their nature. You may *voluntarily* plant in your subconscious mind any plan, thought, or purpose that you desire to translate into its physical or monetary equivalent. The subconscious acts first on the dominating desires that have been mixed with emotional feeling, such as faith.

Consider this in connection with the instructions given in Chapter 1 on desire, for taking the six steps outlined there, and the instructions given in the chapter on building plans, and you will understand the importance of the thought conveyed.

The subconscious mind works day and night.

Through a method of procedure, unknown to humankind, the subconscious mind draws on the forces of Infinite Intelligence for the power with which it voluntarily transmutes someone's desires into their physical equivalent, making use always of the most practical media by which this end is accomplished.

You cannot entirely control your subconscious mind, but you can voluntarily hand over to it any plan, desire, or purpose that you wish transformed into concrete form. Read again instructions for using the subconscious mind in Chapter 3 on auto-suggestion.

There is plenty of evidence to support the belief that the subconscious mind is the connecting link between the finite mind of humans and Infinite Intelligence. It is the intermediary through which we can draw on the forces of Infinite Intelligence at will. It, alone, contains the secret process by which mental impulses are modified and changed into their spiritual equivalent. It, alone, is the medium through which prayer may be transmitted to the Source capable of answering prayer.

The possibilities of creative effort connected with the subconscious mind are stupendous and imponderable. They inspire us with awe.

I never approach the discussion of the subconscious mind without a feeling of littleness and inferiority due, perhaps, to the fact that our entire stock of knowledge on this subject is so pitifully limited. The very fact that the subconscious mind is the medium of communication between the thinking mind of humans and Infinite Intelligence is, of itself, a thought that almost paralyzes a person's reason.

After you have accepted as reality the existence of the subconscious mind and understand its possibilities as a medium for transmuting your desires into their physical or monetary equivalent, you will comprehend the full significance of the instructions given in Chapter 1 on desire. You will also understand why you have been repeatedly admonished to *make your desires clear and reduce them to writing*. You will also understand the necessity of *persistence* in carrying out instructions.

The thirteen principles, or steps, are the stimuli with which you acquire the ability to reach and to influence your subconscious mind. Do not become discouraged if you cannot do this on the first attempt. Remember that the subconscious mind may be voluntarily directed only through habit, under the directions given in Chapter 2 on faith. You have not yet had time to master faith. Be patient. Be persistent.

Do not become discouraged. Be patient. Be persistent.

A good many statements in the chapters on faith and auto-suggestion will be repeated here, for the benefit of your subconscious mind. Remember, your subconscious mind functions voluntarily, whether you make any effort to influence it or not. This, naturally, suggests to you that thoughts of fear and poverty and all negative thoughts serve as stimuli to your subconscious mind—unless you master these impulses and give it more desirable food on which to feed.

The subconscious mind will not remain idle! *If you fail to plant desires* in your subconscious mind, it will feed on the thoughts that reach it as the result of your neglect. We have already explained that thought impulses, both negative and positive, are reaching the subconscious mind continuously from the four sources mentioned in the Sex Transmutation chapter.

For the present, it is sufficient if you remember that you are living daily in the midst of all manner of thought impulses that are reaching your subconscious mind, without your knowledge. Some of these impulses are negative, some are positive. You are now engaged in trying to shut off the flow of negative impulses and purposely influencing your subconscious mind through positive impulses of positive and deliberate desire.

When you achieve this, you will possess the key that unlocks the door to your subconscious mind. Moreover, you will control that door so completely that no undesirable thought will influence your subconscious mind.

Control your mind so no undesirable thought will enter your subconscious mind.

The subconscious mind is more susceptible to influence by impulses of thought mixed with "feeling" or emotion than by those originating solely in the reasoning portion of the mind. In fact, there is much evidence to support the theory that *only* emotionalized thoughts have any *action influence* on the subconscious mind. It is a well-known fact that emotion, or feeling, rules the majority of people.

If it is true that the subconscious mind responds more quickly to, and is influenced more readily by, thought impulses that are well mixed with emotion, it is essential to become familiar with the more important of the emotions. There are seven major positive emotions, and seven major negative emotions. The negatives voluntarily inject themselves into the thought impulses, which ensure passage into the subconscious mind. The positives must be injected through the principle of auto-suggestion, into the thought impulses that we want to pass on to our subconscious mind. (Instructions have been given in Chapter 3 on auto-suggestion.)

These emotions, or feeling impulses, may be likened to yeast in a loaf of bread, because they constitute the *action* element, which transforms thought impulses from the passive to the active state. Thus we can understand why thought impulses, which have been well mixed with emotion, are acted upon more readily than thought impulses originating in "cold reason."

You are preparing yourself to influence and control the "inner audience" of your subconscious mind in order to hand over to it the desire for success, which you wish transmuted into its monetary equivalent. It is essential, therefore, that you understand the method of approach to this "inner audience." You must speak its language, or it will not heed your call. It understands best the language of emotion or feeling.

Let's examine the seven major positive emotions and the seven major negative emotions, so you may draw on the positives and avoid the negatives when giving instructions to your subconscious mind.

The Seven Major Positive Emotions

1. Desire

2. Faith

3. Love

4. Sex

5. Enthusiasm

6. Romance

7. Hope

There are other positive emotions, but these are the seven most powerful, and the ones most commonly used in creative effort. Master these seven emotions (they can be mastered only by *use),* and the other positive emotions will be at your command when you need them. You are studying a book intended to help you develop a "money consciousness" by filling your mind with positive emotions. You will not become money conscious by filling your mind with negative emotions.

The Seven Major Negative Emotions—to be avoided

1. Fear

2. Jealousy

3. Hatred

4. Revenge

5. Greed

6. Superstition

7. Anger

Positive and negative emotions cannot occupy the mind at the same time. One or the other must dominate. It is your responsibility to make sure that positive emotions constitute the dominating influence of your mind. Here the law of *habit* will come to your aid. **Form the habit of applying and using positive emotions!** Eventually, they will dominate your mind so completely that the negatives cannot enter.

Only by following this process literally and continuously can you gain control over your subconscious mind. The presence of a single negative in your conscious mind is sufficient to destroy all chances of constructive aid from your subconscious mind.

IMPORTANT SUMMARY POINTS

- You cannot entirely control your subconscious mind, but you can voluntarily hand over to it any plan, desire, or purpose you wish to transform into a concrete form.

- The possibilities of creative effort connected with the subconscious mind are stupendous.

- Don't be discouraged if you cannot control your subconscious the first time you try. It can only be directed through habit.

- Remember, your subconscious mind functions voluntarily whether you make any effort to influence it or not.

- Negative thoughts serve as stimuli to your subconscious mind, unless you master these impulses and give it more desirable food.

TAKE ACTION

The following are important, major attributes of leadership. Select seven of these attributes and decide to make them a daily habit—part of your mindset and lifestyle.

☐ *Unwavering courage* based upon knowledge of self and your occupation. No follower wishes to be dominated by a leader who lacks self-confidence and courage. No intelligent follower will be dominated by such a leader very long.

☐ *Self-control.* People who cannot control themselves can never control others. Self-control sets a mighty example for your followers, which the more intelligent will emulate.

☐ *A keen sense of justice.* Without a sense of fairness and justice, no leader can command and retain the respect of the followers.

☐ *Definiteness of decision.* Those who waver in decisions show that they are not sure of themselves. They cannot lead others successfully.

☐ *Definiteness of plans.* Successful leaders must plan their work, and work their plan. Leaders who move by guesswork, without practical, definite plans, is comparable to a ship without a rudder. Sooner or later they will land on the rocks.

☐ *The habit of doing more than paid for doing.* One of the penalties of leadership is the necessity of willingness, on the part of the leader, to do more than required of the followers.

☐ *A pleasing personality.* No slovenly, careless person can become a successful leader. Leadership calls for respect. Followers will not respect a leader who does not grade high on all the factors of a pleasing personality.

☐ *Sympathy and understanding.* The successful leader must be in sympathy with the followers. Moreover, good leaders must understand them and their problems.

☐ *Mastery of detail.* Successful leadership calls for mastery of details of the leader's position.

☐ *Willingness to assume full responsibility.* The successful leader must be willing to assume responsibility for the mistakes and the shortcomings of the followers. If a leader tries to shift this responsibility, he or she will not remain the leader. If one of the followers makes a mistake and is shown incompetent, the leader must accept that as a failure for hiring such a person.

☐ *Cooperation.* The successful leader must understand and apply the principle of cooperative effort and be able to induce the followers to do the same. *Leadership calls for power, and power calls for cooperation.*

Chapter 12

THE BRAIN:
TWELFTH STEP TOWARD RICHES

The Brain: A Broadcasting and Receiving Station for Thought

When working in conjunction with the late Dr. Alexander Graham Bell and Dr. Elmer R. Gates, I observed that every human brain is both a broadcasting and receiving station for the vibration of thought.

Through the medium of the ether, in a fashion similar to that employed by the radio broadcasting principle, every human brain is capable of picking up vibrations of thought that are being released by other brains.

In connection with the statement in the preceding paragraph, compare and consider the description of the Creative Imagination, as outlined in Chapter 5 on Imagination. The Creative Imagination is the "receiving set" of the brain that receives thoughts released by the brains of others. It is the agency of communication between our conscious, or reasoning mind, and the four sources from which we may receive thought stimuli.

When stimulated, or "stepped up" to a high rate of vibration, the mind becomes more receptive to the vibration of thought that reaches it through the ether from outside sources. This "stepping up" process takes place through positive emotions, or negative emotions. Through the emotions, the vibrations of thought may be increased.

Vibrations of an exceedingly high rate are the only vibrations picked up and carried by the ether from one brain to another. Thought is energy traveling at an exceedingly high rate of vibration. Thought, which has been modified or "stepped up" by any of the major emotions, vibrates at a much higher rate than ordinary thought, and it is this type of thought that passes from one brain to another, through the broadcasting machinery of the human brain.

Thought is energy traveling at an exceedingly high rate of vibration.

The emotion of sex stands at the head of the list of human emotions, as far as intensity and driving force are concerned. The brain stimulated by the emotion of sex vibrates at a much more rapid rate than it does when that emotion is quiescent or absent.

The result of sex transmutation is the increase of the rate of vibration of thoughts to such a pitch that the Creative Imagination becomes highly receptive to ideas, which it picks up from the ether. On the other hand, when the brain is vibrating at a rapid rate, it not only attracts thoughts and ideas released by other brains through the medium of the ether, but it gives to our own thoughts that "feeling" that is essential before those thoughts will be picked up and acted on by our subconscious mind.

Thus, you will see that the broadcasting principle is the factor through which you mix feeling, or emotion with your thoughts and pass them on to your subconscious mind.

The subconscious mind is the "sending station" of the brain, through which vibrations of thought are broadcast. The Creative Imagination is the "receiving set," through which the vibrations of thought are picked up from the ether.

Along with the important factors of the subconscious mind and the faculty of the Creative Imagination, which constitute the sending and receiving sets of your mental broadcasting machinery, consider now the principle of auto-suggestion, which is the medium by which you may put into operation your "broadcasting" station.

Through the instructions described in Chapter 3 on auto-suggestion, you were definitely informed of the method by which desire may be transmuted into its monetary equivalent.

Operation of your mental "broadcasting" station is a comparatively simple procedure. You have three principles to bear in mind and apply when you wish to use your broadcasting station: 1) the subconscious mind; 2) creative imagination; and 3) auto-suggestion. The stimuli through which you put these three principles into action have been described—the procedure begins with desire.

If you understand the principle described in Chapter 9 on the Master Mind, you of course recognize the round-table procedure here described as being a practical application of the Master Mind.

This method of mind stimulation, through harmonious discussion of definite subjects between three people, illustrates the simplest and most practical use of the Master Mind.

By adopting and following a similar plan, any student of this philosophy may come into possession of the famous Carnegie formula briefly described in previous chapters.

IMPORTANT SUMMARY POINTS

- Every human brain is both a broadcasting and receiving station for the vibration of thought.

- The Creative Imagination is the "receiving set" of the brain, which receives thoughts released by the brains of others.

- Through the emotions, the vibrations of thought may be increased.

- The brain that has been stimulated by the emotion of sex vibrates at a much more rapid rate than it does when that emotion is dormant or absent.

- The broadcasting principle is the factor through which you mix feeling or emotion with your thoughts and pass them on to your subconscious mind.

TAKE ACTION

The following is a self-analysis designed to help you examine aspects of yourself that you may take for granted or have never really thought about previously as being important to who you really are, where you really want to go, and what you really want to accomplish in life. Seriously consider each question, answer it, and then take action as soon as possible.

1. Have I *attained the goal* I established as my objective for this year? (You should work with a definite yearly objective to be attained as part of your major life objective.) Write down your yearly objective and describe the details of your success or failure in attaining this goal.

_____

_____

_____

_____

_____

_____

_____

_____

2. Have I delivered a service or products of the best possible *quality,* or could I have improved any part? Write down the evidence of your success or failure in this area and, finally, the ways you can improve the quality of service.

_____

_____

_____

_____

_____

_____

_____

3. Have I delivered service in the greatest possible *quantity* of which I was capable? Write down two ways in which you could improve the quantity of your products or service.

_____

_____

_____

_____

4. Has the *spirit of my conduct* been harmonious and cooperative at all times? Give one example of success in this area and one example of failure. Write down two ways to improve teamwork within your company.

5. Have I permitted the habit of *procrastination* to decrease my efficiency; and if so, to what extent? Write about one method of reducing procrastination while improving efficiency.

6. Have I improved my *personality;* and if so, in what ways? What part of your personality still needs to be improved and why?

7. Have I been *persistent* in following my plans through to completion? What are two examples of your persistence in the face of difficulty or obstacles?

8. Have I reached *decisions promptly and definitely* on all occasions? Give an example of a time you made a prompt decision and it positively affected your business or work.

9. Have I permitted any one or more of the six basic *fears* (discussed in Chapter 14) to decrease my efficiency? What will you do to confront that fear moving forward?

_____

_____

_____

_____

_____

10. Have I been either "overcautious," or "under-cautious?" Give an example of each in your work and write down your idea of what you will do next time.

_____

_____

_____

_____

_____

_____

_____

11. Has my _relationship_ with my associates been pleasant or unpleasant? If unpleasant, has the fault been partly or wholly mine? Reflect on your work relationships and write down the details of a key relationship that needs improvement.

_____

_____

_____

_____

_____
_____
_____
_____
_____

12. Have I dissipated any of my energy through lack of _concentration_ of effort? Write down your assessment of your ability to concentrate.

_____
_____
_____
_____
_____
_____
_____
_____

13. Have I been _open-minded and tolerant_ in connection with all subjects? What is one subject that causes you to shut down or close your mind to possibilities?

_____
_____
_____
_____
_____
_____

14. In what way have I *improved* my ability to render service? Write down a key area of improvement within your company or workspace.

_____

_____

_____

_____

_____

_____

_____

_____

15. Have I been *intemperate* in any of my habits? Write down some bad habits that you are trying to overcome. What will you replace them with?

_____

_____

_____

_____

_____

_____

_____

_____

_____

16. Have I expressed, either openly or secretly, any form of _egotism_? Write down two ways in which an inflated sense of self-importance can detract from your business or work.

_____

_____

_____

_____

_____

_____

_____

_____

_____

17. Has my _conduct_ toward my associates induced them to _respect_ me? Write down two reasons you feel that your associates respect you. What part of your conduct might cause a lack of respect?

_____

_____

_____

_____

_____

_____

_____

_____

_____

_____

_____

18. Have my opinions and *decisions* been based on guesswork, or accuracy of analysis and *thought*? Write down an example of a decision-making process that brought successful results. How can you replicate this?

_____

_____

_____

_____

_____

_____

_____

_____

19. Have I followed the *habit of budgeting* my time, expenses, and income, and have I been conservative in these budgets? Are you more successful managing your time than your finances? The opposite? What can you do to improve management of both of these key areas of your life?

_____

_____

_____
_____
_____
_____
_____
_____
_____
_____

20. How much time have I devoted to _unprofitable_ effort that I might have used to better advantage? Write down two work or business endeavors that you now see as time wasted. What would you do differently next time?

_____
_____
_____
_____
_____
_____
_____
_____
_____
_____

21. How may I *re-budget* my time and change my habits so I will be more efficient during the coming year? Write down one habit that you consider a time waster in your life that you can overcome. How will you overcome it?

_____

_____

_____

_____

_____

_____

_____

_____

22. Have I been guilty of any *conduct* not approved by my conscience? Is there something about the way you are living that you are not at peace with? What will you do to change it?

_____

_____

_____

_____

_____

_____

_____

23. In what ways have I rendered *more service and better service* than I was paid to render? Write down two examples of going above and beyond.

_____

_____

_____

_____

_____

_____

_____

_____

_____

_____

24. Have I been *unfair* to anyone; if so, in what way? Write down the details of the situation and what you can/did do to make it right.

_____

_____

_____

_____

_____

_____

_____

25. If I had been the purchaser of my own services for the year, would I be *satisfied* with my purchase? Write a review of your product or service as if you were a paying customer.

_____

_____

_____

_____

_____

_____

_____

_____

_____

26. Am I in the right vocation; and if not, why not? If you are in the right vocation, write down the details of how you know this.

_____

_____

_____

_____

_____

_____

_____

_____

_____

_____

_____

_____

_____

27. Has the purchaser of my services been satisfied with the service I have rendered; if not, why not? Write down a received complaint and compliment of your service or product.

_____

_____

_____

_____

_____

_____

_____

_____

_____

_____

_____

_____

_____

Chapter 13

THE SIXTH SENSE:
THIRTEENTH STEP TOWARD RICHES

The Sixth Sense: The Door to the Temple of Wisdom

The thirteenth principle is known as the sixth sense, through which Infinite Intelligence may and will communicate voluntarily, without any effort from or demands by the individual. This principle is the apex of the philosophy. It can be assimilated, understood, and applied *only* by first mastering the other twelve principles.

The sixth sense is that portion of the subconscious mind referred to as the Creative Imagination. It has also been referred to as the "receiving set" through which ideas, plans, and thoughts flash into the mind. The "flashes" are sometimes called "hunches" or "inspirations."

The sixth sense defies description! It cannot be described to a person who has not mastered the other principles of this philosophy, because such a person has no knowledge and no experience with which the sixth sense may be compared. Understanding of the sixth sense comes only by meditation through mind development from within.

The sixth sense probably is the medium of contact between the finite mind of humans and Infinite Intelligence; and for this reason, it is a mixture of both the mental and the spiritual. It is believed to be the point at which the minds of humans contact the Universal Mind.

> **Through the sixth sense, you will be warned of dangers in time to avoid them and notified of opportunities in time to embrace them.**

After you have mastered the principles described in this *Think and Grow Rich* workbook, you will be prepared to accept as truth a statement which may otherwise be incredible to you, namely: Through the aid of the sixth sense, you will be warned of impending dangers in time to avoid them and notified of opportunities in time to embrace them.

There comes to your aid, and to do your bidding with the development of the sixth sense, a "guardian angel" who will open to you at all times the door to the "Temple of Wisdom."

Whether or not this is a statement of truth, you will never know, except by following the instructions described in the pages of this workbook, or some similar method of procedure.

The author is not a believer in, nor an advocate of "miracles," for the reason that he has enough knowledge of Nature to understand that Nature never deviates from her established laws. Some of her laws are so incomprehensible that they produce what appears to be "miracles." The sixth sense comes as near to being a miracle as anything I have ever experienced, and it appears so, only because I do not understand the method by which this principle is operated.

This much the author does know—that there is a power, or a First Cause, or an Intelligence that permeates every atom of matter and embraces every unit of energy perceptible to humanity—that this Infinite Intelligence converts acorns into oak trees, causes water to flow downhill in response to the law of gravity, follows night with day, and winter with summer, each maintaining its proper place and relationship to the other. This Intelligence may, through the principles of this philosophy, be induced to aid in transmuting desires into concrete or material form. The author has this knowledge because he has experimented with it—and has *experienced it*.

Step by step, through the preceding chapters, you have been led to this, the last principle. If you have mastered each of the preceding principles, you are now prepared to accept, without being skeptical, the stupendous claims made here. If you have not mastered the other principles, you must do so before you can definitely determine whether or not the claims made in this chapter are fact or fiction.

The sixth sense is not something that you can take off and put on at will. Ability to use this great power comes slowly, through application of the other principles outlined in this workbook. Seldom does any individual come into workable knowledge of the sixth sense before the age of forty. More often the knowledge is not available until one is well past fifty, and this, for the reason that the spiritual forces with which the sixth sense is so closely related, do not mature and become usable except through years of meditation, self-examination, and serious thought.

The chapter on the sixth sense was included because the *Think and Grow Rich* book is designed for the purpose of presenting a complete philosophy by which individuals may unerringly guide themselves in attaining whatever they ask of life. The starting point of all achievement is desire. The finishing point is the brand of knowledge that leads to understanding—understanding of self, understanding of others, understanding of the laws of Nature, recognition and understanding of happiness.

IMPORTANT SUMMARY POINTS

- The sixth sense is the portion of the subconscious mind referred to as Creative Imagination.

- Understanding the sixth sense comes only by meditation through mind development from within.

- The sixth sense is a mixture of both the mental and the spiritual.

- The sixth sense is not something that you can take off and put on at will. Ability to use this great power comes slowly, through application of the other twelve principles, or steps.

TAKE ACTION

The following is a comprehensive list of over fifty questions that delve deeply into your being. Plan a full day of quiet reflection alone to answer all the questions truthfully and completely. When finished, you will have an all-inclusive look into your soul, which will help you in your goal to *think and grow rich* in all aspects of your life.

1. Do you complain often of "feeling badly"? If so, what is the cause? What are some ways to make yourself feel better?

_____

_____

_____

_____

_____

_____

_____

_____

_____

_____

_____

2. Do you find fault with other people at the slightest provocation? What are some ways you can work to change this impulse?

_____

_____

_____

_____

_____

_____

_____

_____

_____

_____

_____

3. Do you frequently make mistakes in your work? If so, why?

_____

_____

_____

_____
_____
_____
_____
_____
_____
_____
_____
_____
_____
_____
_____

4. Is your conversation sarcastic and offensive?

_____
_____
_____
_____
_____
_____
_____
_____
_____
_____

5. Do you deliberately avoid associating with anyone? If so, why?

6. Does life seem futile and the future hopeless? If so, why?

_____
_____
_____
_____
_____
_____
_____
_____
_____
_____
_____
_____

7. Do you like your occupation? If not, why?

_____
_____
_____
_____
_____

_____

_____

_____

_____

_____

_____

_____

_____

8. Do you often feel self-pity? If so, why?

_____

_____

_____

_____

_____

_____

_____

_____

_____

_____

_____
_____
_____

9. Are you envious of those who excel you?

_____
_____
_____
_____
_____
_____
_____
_____
_____
_____
_____
_____

10. To which do you devote the most time thinking about—success or failure?

_____
_____
_____

_____

_____

_____

_____

_____

_____

_____

_____

_____

_____

11. Are you gaining or losing self-confidence as you grow older?

_____

_____

_____

_____

_____

_____

_____

12. Do you learn something of value from all mistakes?

13. Are you permitting some relative or acquaintance to worry you? If so, why?

_____

_____

_____

_____

_____

_____

_____

_____

_____

_____

_____

14. Are you sometimes "in the clouds" and at other times in the "depths of despondency"?

_____

_____

_____

_____

15. Who has the most inspiring influence on you?

16. What is the cause of that inspiration?

17. Do you tolerate negative or discouraging influences that you can avoid?

_____

_____

_____

_____

_____

_____

_____

_____

_____

_____

18. Are you careless with your personal appearance? If so, when and why?

_____

_____

_____

_____

_____

_____

_____

_____

_____

_____

_____

_____

_____

_____

19. Have you learned how to "drown your troubles" by being too busy to be annoyed by them?

_____

_____

_____

_____

_____

_____

_____

_____

_____

_____

_____

_____

20. Do you ever permit others to think for you?

_____

_____

_____

_____

_____

_____

_____

_____

_____

_____

_____

21. Do you neglect internal renewal until auto-intoxication makes you ill-tempered and irritable?

_____

_____

_____

_____

22. How many preventable disturbances annoy you? Why do you tolerate them?

23. Do you resort to liquor, narcotics, or cigarettes to "quiet your nerves"? If so, why not try willpower instead?

24. Does anyone "nag" you? If so, for what reason?

_____

_____

_____

_____

_____

_____

_____

_____

_____

_____

_____

25. Do you have a definite major purpose? If so, what is it, and what plan have you for achieving it?

_____

_____

_____

_____

_____

_____

_____

_____

_____

_____

_____

_____

_____

26. Do you suffer from any of the six basic fears (discussed in Chapter 14)? If so, which ones?

_____

_____

_____

_____

_____

_____

_____

_____

_____

_____

_____

_____

_____

_____

27. Do you have a method to shield yourself against the negative influence of others?

_____

_____

_____

_____

_____

_____

_____

_____

_____

_____

_____

28. Do you make deliberate use of auto-suggestion to ensure a positive mindset?

_____

_____

_____

----

29. Which do you value most—your material possessions or the privilege of controlling your thoughts?

----

30. Are you easily influenced by others, against your own judgment?

31. Has today added anything of value to your stock of knowledge or state of mind?

_____

_____

_____

_____

_____

_____

_____

_____

_____

_____

_____

_____

32. Do you face squarely the circumstances that make you unhappy, or sidestep the responsibility?

_____

_____

_____

_____

_____

_____

_____

_____

_____

_____

_____

33. Do you analyze all mistakes and failures and try to profit by them, or do you think that is not your duty?

_____

_____

_____

_____

_____

_____

_____

_____

_____

_____

_____

34. Name three of your most damaging weaknesses? What are you doing to correct them?

35. Do you encourage other people to bring their worries to you for sympathy?

_____

_____

_____

_____

_____

_____

_____

_____

_____

_____

_____

36. Do you choose, from your daily experiences, lessons or influences that aid your personal advancement?

_____

_____

_____

_____

_____

_____

_____

_____

_____

_____

_____

_____

_____

37. Does your presence have a negative or positive influence on other people?

_____

_____

_____

_____

_____

_____

_____

_____

_____

_____

_____

_____

---

38. If you believe that "birds of a feather flock together," what have you learned about yourself by studying the friends whom you attract?

---

39. What connection, if any, do you see between the people with whom you closely associate and any unhappiness you may experience?

---

40. By what rules do you judge who is helpful and who is damaging to you?

41. Are your intimate associates mentally superior or inferior to you?

42. How much time out of every twenty-four hours do you devote to:

    your occupation _____

    sleep _____

    play and relaxation _____

    acquiring useful knowledge _____

    TV, social media _____

43. Who among your acquaintances:

    encourages you most

    _____

    _____

    _____

    cautions you most

    _____

    _____

    _____

    discourages you most

    _____

    _____

    _____

    helps you most in other ways

    _____

    _____

44. What is your greatest worry? Why do you tolerate it?

45. When others offer you free, unsolicited advice, do you accept it without question, or do you analyze their motives?

---

46. What, above all else, do you most desire?

_____
_____
_____
_____
_____
_____

47. How do you intend to acquire it?

_____
_____
_____
_____
_____
_____
_____
_____
_____
_____
_____
_____
_____
_____

48. Are you willing to subordinate all other desires for this one?

_____

_____
_____
_____
_____
_____
_____
_____
_____
_____
_____
_____
_____

49. How much time daily do you devote to acquiring it?

_____
_____
_____
_____
_____
_____

_____

_____

_____

_____

_____

_____

50. Do you change your mind often? If so, why?

_____

_____

_____

_____

_____

_____

_____

_____

_____

_____

_____

_____

51. Do you usually finish everything you begin?

52. Are you easily impressed by other people's business or professional titles, college degrees, or wealth?

53. Are you easily influenced by what other people think or say about you?

54. Do you cater to people because of their social or financial status?

55. Whom do you believe to be the greatest person living?

_____

_____

_____

_____

_____

_____

_____

_____

_____

_____

_____

56. In what respect is this person superior to you?

_____

_____

_____

_____

_____

_____

_57._ How much time have you devoted to studying and answering these questions? Was that enough? Should you review some, most, or all of the questions and answers?

Chapter 14

HOW TO OUTWIT THE SIX GHOSTS OF FEAR

Take Inventory of Yourself

Before you can put any portion of this philosophy into successful use, your mind must be prepared to receive it. The preparation is not difficult. It begins with study, analysis, and understanding of three enemies that you have to *clear out of your mind: indecision, doubt, and fear!*

Your sixth sense will never function while these three negatives, or any one of them, remain in your mind. The members of this unholy trio are closely related; where one is found, the other two are close at hand.

Indecision is the seedling of fear! Remember that indecision crystallizes into doubt, the two blend and become fear! The "blending" process often is slow. This is one reason why these three enemies are so dangerous. They germinate and grow without their presence being observed.

The purpose of this chapter is to turn the spotlight on the cause and the cure of the six basic fears. Before we can master an enemy, we must know its name, its habits, and its place of abode. As you read, analyze yourself carefully and determine which, if any, of the six common fears have attached to you.

Do not be deceived by the habits of these subtle enemies. Sometimes they remain hidden in the subconscious mind where they are difficult to locate, and still more difficult to eliminate.

The Six Basic Fears

There are six basic fears that every human suffers from at one time or another. Most people are fortunate if they do not suffer from the entire six. Named in the order of their most common appearance, they are the fears of:

1. Poverty

2. Criticism

3. Ill health

4. Loss of someone's love

5. Old age

6. Death

All other fears are of minor importance and can be grouped under these six headings.

The prevalence of these fears, as a curse to the world, runs in cycles. For almost six years, during the Great Depression, many floundered in the cycle of the fear of poverty. During the World Wars, many lived in the cycle of the fear of death. Following wars, many live in the cycle of the fear of ill health, evidenced by the epidemic of diseases worldwide.

Fears are nothing more than states of mind. Our states of mind are subject to control and direction. It's been said that physicians are less subject to attack by disease than other people because physicians do not fear disease. Without fear or hesitation they have been known to physically contact hundreds of people, daily, who are suffering from such contagious diseases, yet do not become infected. Their immunity against the disease consists, largely, if not solely, in their lack of fear.

Humans can create nothing that they do not first conceive in the form of an impulse of thought. Following this statement comes another of still greater importance: *Our thought impulses begin immediately to translate into a physical equivalent, whether those thoughts are voluntary or involuntary.* Thought impulses picked up through the ether, by mere chance (thoughts that have been released by other minds), may determine your financial, business, professional, or social destiny just as surely as do the thought impulses that we create by intent and design.

We are here laying the foundation for the presentation of a fact of great importance to the person who does not understand why some people appear to be "lucky" while others of equal or greater ability, training, experience, and brain capacity seem destined to ride with misfortune. This fact may be explained by the statement that *every human being has the ability to completely control their own minds; and with this control, obviously, every person may open their minds to the negative thought impulses being released by other brains, or close the doors tightly and admit only thought impulses of their own choice.*

Nature has endowed us with absolute control over only one thing: thought. This fact, coupled with the additional fact that everything that we create begins in the form of a thought, leads us very near to the principle by which fear may be mastered.

If it is true that *all thought has a tendency to clothe itself in its physical equivalent* (this is true beyond any reasonable room for doubt), it is equally true that thought impulses of fear and poverty cannot be translated into terms of courage and financial gain.

The six basic fears become translated into a state of worry through indecision. Take these steps to overcome fears:

- Relieve yourself forever of the fear of death by deciding to accept death as an inescapable event.

- Whip the fear of poverty by reaching a decision to get along with whatever wealth you can accumulate *without worry.*

- Put your foot upon the neck of the fear of criticism by deciding not to worry about what other people think, do, or say.

- Eliminate the fear of old age by deciding to accept it, not as a handicap, but as a great blessing that carries with it wisdom, self-control, and understanding not known to youth.

- Acquit yourself of the fear of ill health by deciding to forget symptoms.

- Master the fear of loss of love by deciding to get along without love, if that is necessary.

Kill the habit of worry, in all its forms, by reaching a general, blanket decision that nothing life has to offer is worth the price of worry. With this decision comes poise, peace of mind, and calmness of thought that will bring happiness.

A person's whose mind is filled with fear not only destroys his or her chances of intelligent action, but transmits these destructive vibrations to the minds of all with whom they come into contact.

IMPORTANT SUMMARY POINTS

- Before you can put this philosophy into successful use, you must clear your mind of three enemies: indecision, doubt, and fear.

- Indecision is the seedling of fear. It crystallizes into doubt and the two blend and become fear.

- There are six basic fears: poverty, criticism, ill health, loss of someone's love, old age, and death.

- Fears are nothing more than states of mind that can be altered and eliminated.

TAKE ACTION

The following are fifty-seven "Famous Alibis by Old Man If." As you read each one, make a mark by the one(s) you have used as an alibi for not being as successful or as happy as you could be.

- [ ] **IF** I didn't have a wife and family...

- [ ] **IF** I had enough "pull"...

- [ ] **IF** I had money...

- [ ] **IF** I had a good education...

- [ ] **IF** I could get a job...

- [ ] **IF** I had good health...

- [ ] **IF** I only had time...

- [ ] **IF** times were better...

- [ ] **IF** other people understood me...

☐ **IF** conditions around me were different…

☐ **IF** I could live my life over again…

☐ **IF** I did not fear what "they" would say…

☐ **IF** I had been given a chance…

☐ **IF** I only had a chance…

☐ **IF** other people didn't have it in for me…

☐ **IF** nothing happens to stop me…

☐ **IF** I were only younger…

☐ **IF** I could only do what I want…

☐ **IF** I had been born rich…

☐ **IF** I could meet the right people…

☐ **IF** I had the talent that some people have…

☐ **IF** I dared assert myself…

☐ **IF** I only had embraced past opportunities…

☐ **IF** people didn't get on my nerves…

☐ **IF** I didn't have to keep house and look after the children…

☐ **IF** I could save some money…

☐ **IF** the boss appreciated me…

☐ **IF** I only had somebody to help me…

☐ **IF** my family understood me...

☐ **IF** I lived in a big city...

☐ **IF** I could just get started...

☐ **IF** I were free...

☐ **IF** I had the personality of some people...

☐ **IF** I were not so fat...

☐ **IF** my talents were known...

☐ **IF** I could just get a break...

☐ **IF** I could only get out of debt...

☐ **IF** I hadn't failed...

☐ **IF** I only knew how...

☐ **IF** everybody didn't oppose me...

☐ **IF** I didn't have so many worries...

☐ **IF** I could marry the right person...

☐ **IF** people weren't so dumb...

☐ **IF** my family were not so extravagant...

☐ **IF** I were sure of myself...

☐ **IF** luck were not against me...

☐ **IF** I had not been born under the wrong star...

☐ **IF** it were not true that what will be will be…

☐ **IF** I did not have to work so hard…

☐ **IF** I hadn't lost my money…

☐ **IF** I lived in a different neighborhood…

☐ **IF** I didn't have a past…

☐ **IF** I only had a business of my own…

☐ **IF** other people would only listen to me…

☐ **IF**—and this is the greatest excuse of them all—**IF** I had the courage to see myself as I really am, I would find out what is wrong with me and correct it, then I might have a chance to profit from my mistakes and learn something from the experience of others, for I know that there is something wrong with me, or I would now be where I would have been IF I had spent more time analyzing my weaknesses, and less time building alibis to cover them.

Building alibis is a deeply rooted habit. Habits are difficult to break, especially when they provide justification for something we do. Plato had this truth in mind when he said, "The first and best victory is to conquer self. To be conquered by self is, of all things, the most shameful and vile."

CONCLUSION

THE AUTHOR DISCOVERED, THROUGH personally analyzing hundreds of successful people, that all of them followed the habit of exchanging ideas. When they had problems to be solved, they sat down together and talked freely until they discovered, from their joint contribution of ideas, a plan that would serve their purpose.

You will get most out of what you learned in this workbook by putting into practice the Master Mind principle. This you can do (as others are doing so successfully) by forming a study club consisting of any desired number of people who are friendly and harmonious. The club should meet regularly, as often as once each week, and should consist of reading one chapter of *Think and Grow Rich* at each meeting and discussing the contents freely by all members. Each person should take notes, writing ideas that come to mind inspired by the discussion.

Prior to each meeting, members should carefully read and complete the corresponding chapter in this workbook. It should be decided by the group members if everyone will share their answers in the workbook or limit discussion to the book.

By following this plan, you will benefit not only from the sum total of the best knowledge organized from the experiences of hundreds of successful men, but more important by far, you will tap new sources of knowledge in your own mind as well as acquire knowledge of priceless value from others present.

Riches cannot always be measured in money!

Remember, riches cannot always be measured in money! Money and material things are essential for freedom of body and mind, but there are some who will feel that the greatest of all riches can be evaluated only in terms of lasting friendships, harmonious family relationships, sympathy and measurable only in spiritual values!

Nevertheless, if you understand and apply the thirteen steps and adopt this philosophy, you will be better prepared to attract and enjoy higher estates that always have been and always will be denied to all except those who are ready for them.

Be prepared, therefore, when you expose yourself to the influence of this philosophy to experience a changed life that can help you not only to negotiate your way through life with harmony and understanding, but also prepare you for the accumulation of material riches in abundance!

NOTES